WYRALE

WIRRAL TOPICS

INCLUDING
THE FOREST OF WIRRAL, COUNTRY WOMEN,
THE NEW CUT, DEE FISHERMEN,
NESTON MINERS, HESWALL SLACK,
HILBRE ISLAND AND LITTLE MEOLS.

by
GREG DAWSON

with research by
GERALDINE RYAN

First Published 1996.

Copyright © Greg Dawson 1996

ISBN 0-9522598-2-6

All rights reserved. No part of this book may be reproduced or utilized in any form or by any means, electronic or mechanical, including photocopying, or by any information storage and retrieval system, without permission in writing.

British Library Cataloguing-in-Publication Data.
A catalogue record for this book is available from the British Library.

Published by Dawson Publishing (of Irby).
Printed by INPRINT, King Street, Wallasey.
Typesetting by DAISYWHEEL, Bell Road, Wallasey.

£4.95

ACKNOWLEDGEMENTS

As always, I must first and foremost thank all the "locals" for providing the oral history, anecdotes and traditions of the area. Without their enthusiastic help, much knowledge would be lost.

Thanks also to the Archivists and staff of Cheshire County Council Archives and Local Studies, Birkenhead Reference Library, Liverpool Museum, Liverpool Record Office, Cheshire County Sites and Monuments Records, Flintshire County Council Records Office, Anglesey County Council Record Office and Wrexham Reference Library, for the help and patience of their staff, and permission to use some of the documents from their collections.

Once again special thanks must go to three local historians; my sister Geraldine Ryan, for carrying out so much research for me into census returns and church records and for persuing and solving endless queries, Derek Young, for the illustrations and Jim O'Neil, for his invaluable advice.

Also thanks to people who have passed on documentary information, old newspaper cuttings and family letters etc.; Paul Booth of Liverpool University, Fred Windsor of Bromborough, Charles Williams of Heswall and John Miller formerly of Parkside Colliery, Newton-le-Willows.

I am also very grateful to people who have been kind enough to loan old photographs; Maurice Paul Evans, Derek Young, Ian Boumphrey, Janet Fearne, Edward Hilditch and Alf Oxton, and also to Rolph Jordan who sketched the mining scenes.

Last but not least, to my wife Jenny for putting up with me going missing for hours on end on my days off when we should have been together, and to her friend Dorothy Williams of Irby for her helpful suggestions about my notes.

CONTENTS

THE FOREST OF WIRRAL.	Page 1
WIRRAL COUNTRY WOMEN AT WORK.	10
THE NEW CUT TO CHESTER.	17
THE DEE FISHERMEN.	25
NESTON COAL MINES.	39
HESWALL SLACK.	63
HILBRE ISLANDS.	76
LITTLE MEOLS.	83
INFORMATION & REFERENCES.	94
GLOSSARY.	95
MAPS.	96

COVER PHOTOGRAPH

Fishermen climbing the steps from Caldy Beach, 1965.

Heswall fishermen, the late Henry Evans and his son Henry carrying their catch of shrimps up the steps from Caldy Beach. Henry was a very interesting person to talk to, he was a fisherman all his life apart from serving six years in the Royal Navy during the Second World War. Hilbre Island can be seen in the background. (From the Guyse Williams collection, courtesy John King).

ILLUSTRATIONS.

Page	
7	Storeton Hall.
8	Bidston Hill c 1900.
9	Lower Heath Wood, September 1996.
12	Loading muck at Storeton Hall Farm c.1916.
13	Spreading muck in Storeton fields.
16	Tea break in Landican fields.
16	Alf Oxton and potato pickers.
18	The New Cut, September 1996.
23	Burton Point, September 1996.
23	Burton Point Cliffs, September 1996.
32	The Middle Slip, Parkgate c.1930.
34	The Nancy, 1955.
35	Heswall Shore in the 'Big Freeze', 1963.
38	The Gee Whiz and the Blue Circle.
40	A bottle Mine.
41	'Walking' a coal punt along an underground canal.
47	Hewing coal.
48	Ellis 'Peg Leg' Roberts at Wirral Colliery.
58	The last shift at Wirral Colliery.
62	Denhall Quay, September 1996.
69	Reddy's Butchers Shop, Christmas 1931.
71	Regulars outside the Sandon Arms c.1936.
72	The Sandon Arms and Sandon Terrace, September 1996.
75	Sandy Lane, Heswall, September 1996.
80	Hilbre Island from Red Rocks.
82	An aerial view of Hilbre Islands (© D & M Young)
84	The Kings Gap, Hoylake, September 1996.
86	Red Rocks c 1920.
91	Polly Brandreth at Pont-y-Pant, July 1996.

THE FOREST OF WIRRAL

In Medieval times the word *forest* was a legal term concerned with forest laws and the protection of game. A hunting forest was an uncultivated tract of land, not just an area of trees. It covered a wide variety of land, for example, moor, marsh, heaths, wastes and woods, basically any land not cultivated or farmed. The King could claim any land as his forest but he had to put it in writing.

When an area was declared *forest* or *afforested* as it was said, it did not mean that men were sent out to plant trees. The area just became set aside for hunting by the nobility only. Clearing undergrowth, felling trees, digging marl pits, building houses and cultivating new fields in the forest area was forbidden. When, centuries later, these areas were declared to be no longer forest or *disafforested*, people did not go out and cut all the trees down, it just meant that the forest laws were abolished and some of the waste land could be cultivated and farmed.

Since ancient times Celt, Anglo-Saxon and Viking settlers in Wirral had gradually cut down trees and cleared heathland for livestock grazing and to grow crops. They cleared more land as their villages grew. The forests, woods and areas of waste and commons were hunted by the old Anglo-Saxon kings and nobles who respected their peoples farms and crops.

In the Domesday Book the only village in Wirral recorded as having a large area of woodland was Prenton, the wood being one league long and one league wide. (A league in those days was probably the old French mile measured by 1,500 paces). The only other village known to have had a reasonable area of woodland was Mollington with two acres and possibly Tranmere. There were probably scores of smaller woods and patches of trees scattered across the peninsula.

When the Domesday Book was written in 1086 only about 25 hunting forests were recorded, by 1217 there were nearly 150, including Wirral, Delamere and Macclesfield. By the reign of Henry III practically one third of the kingdom was forest. The forest laws introduced by William the Conqueror put a stop to land clearance and restricted the freedom of the local inhabitants. Certain Normans sometimes thought more of the deer than of their Anglo-Saxon subjects and used the forest laws to exploit them.

Wirral was believed to have been declared a forest or afforested, by Randle de Maschines the Third Earl of Chester between 1120 and 1129. The Anglo-Saxon inhabitants of Wirral were taxed and down-trodden, by the hated Normans. They evaded taxes when they could and opposed everything Norman. Some villages had already been destroyed by 1070 on the orders of William the Conqueror for resisting his occupation.

To Randle, the people of Wirral were a thorn in his side. He is believed to have decided to teach them a lesson by sending in Norman soldiers to burn houses, pull down fences and destroy crops. He then declared Wirral a hunting forest. Many years later it became a Royal Forest. But as time went on and more Norman tenants and under-tenants came to live in Wirral, it was they who suffered most from the restrictions and penalties of the forest laws.

Randle appointed a Master Forester in charge of six under-foresters to patrol the forest and uphold forest laws. The first Master Forester of Wirral was believed to have been Alan Sylvester who was granted the manors of Storeton and Puddington. He was entitled to certain rights including timber and game. The under-foresters were entitled to food and lodging in the villages of Wirral as they patroled the forest. Eventually the villages paid a yearly sum for the upkeep of these men called puture money. The Abbot of Chesters manors in Irby, Eastham, Bromborough and Sutton were exempt from puture payments.

An old document in Cheshire Records Office (1) relating to Irby states that soon after the Norman Conquest the manor or town of Irby was given to the Abbey of St. Werberghs and that; *Randle de Meschines made this town free from finding to the foresters of his forest of Wirrehall. The Abbot of St. Werberghs also claimed the liberty of infantheof, wayfs, strays and the chattels of fugitives and felons & etc. in the manors of Irreby and Girorsby* (Greasby)....(Free from finding meant that the Abbey lands in Irby were free from forest laws. Infantheof was the right of the lord of a manor to punish a thief caught in the manor and fugitives were local criminals on the run).

Nothing was allowed to disturb the breeding and grazing of the deer. Wild boar, hares and game birds were also covered by forest laws. People were not even supposed to cut a branch off a growing tree. Houses and mills built without permission were usually pulled down. Fences had to be kept low enough to allow the free movement of deer. Crops were continually eaten by deer or destroyed by the hunt. If people found deer eating their crops they were not allowed to interfere with them, only foresters could drive them away. By the time the foresters turned up and moved the deer on, it was often too late and the villagers crops were destroyed. This caused great hardship. Also in very severe winters the villagers might be forbidden to graze their animals in the forest so to protect grazing for the deer.

Within the forests were protected breeding enclosures for the deer, called parks. The deer could leap over walls into the parks from specially constructed banks called deer leaps, but they could not jump high enough to get out.

The nobles hunted male deer called stags, bucks or harts in summer and autumn, whilst the female deer called hinds or does were hunted after the breeding season, from September to February.

Peasants from local villages were sometimes called upon to assist the hunt by acting as beaters. When a deer was killed, the upper classes drank wine and ate the venison. They allowed the beaters the 'umbles' which are the heart, liver and entrails. Hence the saying "to eat umble pie".

The Head Forester was in a position to give gifts of deer, exempt people from various forest laws or fine them. Permission to cut timber, quarry, mine and graze farm animals in the forest could be granted as long as it did not interfere with hunting.

Any man found to have illegally killed the kings deer could have his eyes put out and anyone caught in the forest with dogs or bow-and-arrows was likely to be mutilated. As the whole of Wirral was afforested, the people were in fear of forest laws and the special forest courts terrorised them. Even Norman tenants of the powerful Barons who had estates in Wirral had to obey all forest laws.

In Medieval times there was not the variety of dogs that there are today; they were working dogs, usually hounds. These dogs had to be 'lawed' or 'humbled' to slow them down and prevent them from catching the kings deer. To 'law' a dog meant to mutilate a paw, and to 'humble' a dog was to pull out all its claws. All dogs had to be shown to surveyors to prove that they had been lawed or humbled. The surveyors had to be shown that the dogs paw had been cut down enough to pass through a special oval shaped ring. Laws like this were hated by both rich and poor.

Mr. Paul Booth of Liverpool University has deeply researched the Forest Records and the Calendar of the Proceedings of the Court of Wirral Forest. He has kindly allowed me to use some of his notes. There are many examples of people being 'amerced', which in these records meant a fine imposed by the court, and a 'fine' was a negotiated penalty.

The following cases were taken from records of the Court of Survey for the Lawing of Dogs in Wirral Forest, 20 September 1311.

UPTON. *Richard Bondson of Upton has a dog which he did not show to the surveyors but afterwards he took it to Sutton where it was surveyed. For his default in the first instance: Amercement 3 shillings and 4 pence (17p).*

NESTON. *The township of Great Neston contemptuously refused to come before the surveyors: Amercement 6s. 8d. (33p).*

BACKFORD. *William Hugh's son of Backford has a dog insufficiently lawed: Amercement 5s. (25p).* (In this instance the dogs paw would have to be cut and trimmed until it passed through the 'paw gauge').

THINGWALL. *Henry Calfe of Thingwall has a dog which he did not show. It is, therefore, to be accounted as not sufficiently lawed and the penalty of an ox is to be levied.* (The fine of an ox in those days was very heavy, today an ox could cost between £700 and £800).

LANDICAN. *Matthew Landican has a dog which he did not show. It is, therefore, to be accounted as not sufficiently lawed and the penalty of an ox is to be levied.*

MOLLINGTON. *The surveyors present that William Brimstage of Mollington had a dog which he made away with four days before the holding of the court. The penalty of an ox was ordered to be levied. As a result, William comes and says that despite the above allegation, he had had no such dog nor did he fraudulently make away with one. He placed himself upon his country (that is, he elected to be tried by jury). The sheriff was ordered to cause a jury of 12 to appear at the next county court.*

The surveyors present that Adam the carpenter of Mollington commited the same offence, at Whitsun last and, likewise, a jury is to be summoned.

ARROWE. *It was presented, by testimony of Peter Gilbert's son of Lymm, that Thomas son of Richard Prenton of Arrowe has concealed a dog which has been in his possession for one year. Thomas comes and says that he possesses no dog at all. He places himself on his country. The sheriff was ordered to cause a jury of 12 to appear at the next County Court.*

NESS. *The surveyors present that William Newton of Ness has an unlawed dog which he sometimes keeps at Ness and sometimes at Neston, and the penalty of an ox is to be levied. As a result, William comes and claims that no ox ought to be levied since, so he says, he has no dog at Ness or anywhere else. He places himself on his country. The sheriff was ordered to cause a jury of 12 to appear at the next county court.*

DOGS KILLED. *The surveyors present that Robert Coly, William Sutton and Robert Ball's daughter, each had a dog which they killed before the holding of the court. Therefore, let the Assize of the Forest be put into execution and three oxen be levied.*

The above are just a few of the many court cases concerning the lawing of dogs in Wirral. In some instances people, usually the clergy, were acquitted as they had special rights granted by previous kings. The two cases below are examples.

GAYTON. *The surveyors present that Richard Wassa's son, Reeve of Gayton, has two dogs unlawed. As a result, Ranulf Merton (Lord of Gayton) comes and claims to be quit of anything to do with the lawing of dogs in his manor of Gayton by reason of a charter granted by King Edward the III which he says he has in his possession. But because he does not produce it, he is told to produce it at the next County Court, if it should be possible. Because it was discovered at the last Court of Survey, held in Robert Holland's time, it was found that Ranulf was rightfully quit of the lawing of dogs in his manor, he is now acquitted.* (A Reeve was an Official or Steward, a Shire Reeve was a Sheriff).

CALDY. *The surveyors present that the Abbot of Basingwerk had a dog which was not lawed, at Caldy Grange and another at Newbold. The penalty of two oxen was ordered to be levied. As a result, the Abbot comes and claims that no oxen ought to be levied since, so he says, he and all his predecessors, abbots of Basingwerk (near Holywell), all the time that granges have been in their possession, have had unlawed dogs in them both in the times of the Earls of Chester and of the Kings. He placed himself upon his country. The Sheriff was ordered to cause a jury of 12 to appear at the next County Court. Because it was discovered that at the last Court of Survey, held in Robert Hollands time, it was found that the Abbot and his predecessors were rightfully quit of the lawing of dogs in those granges, he is now acquitted.* (Granges were farms belonging to the monks).

Extracts from the Calendar of the Proceedings of the Courts of Wirral Forest list many cases of 'Pleas of Venison', which were offences against deer. Below are some court cases from the year 1284.

PENSBY & BARNSTON. *The foresters present that a female fawn was found dead on the bounds of the lands of Pensby and Barnston and, as a result, their draught beasts were driven to Chester Castle and then bailed until the next forest court by Robert Poole, Ralph Barnston (chaplain) and William Thingwall. Then the two townships came here and gave 5 shillings (25p) pledge for the fawn (which is the rate for females, according to the custom of the forest) since they could not agree on finding the evildoers. They all act as pledges for each other.* (What were in those days the bounds of Pensby and Barnston is today Pensby Road).

BIRKENHEAD. *The Prior of Birkenhead was indicted by a jury of 12 and by villagers for knowingly receiving John Stabule, his servant, who is an evildoer in the forest and for consenting to his evil deeds, and for receiving venison taken by him. John did not come, and the sheriff was ordered to arrest him; he reported he could not be found, and had no goods by which he might be compelled to come; the sheriff was ordered to try again.*

The Prior came and denied it. He then sought another jury, relying on the liberty of the county which all living there have, until now, used and enjoyed. Namely that not withstanding the indictment by the jurers and villagers in respect of evil deeds in the forest against the king's venison, they can claim the right to be tried by another jury.

The jury found that the Prior did not have John in his service when the forest offences were committed by him, nor did he recieve him as an evildoer at any time, nor consent to his evil deeds. He is therefore acquitted.

CAPENHURST. *The forester present that Martin, John Thorald's tenant, killed a fawn on Capenhurst heath on Wednesday 25 June 1281 and carried it to John's house, who received him as well as the said venison. Martin came and defended himself by 'Thwerknik', by the liberty of the county. And so he is acquitted, and the said John likewise.* (The custom of Thwirtnik meant that for certain offences in Cheshire courts, accused people could acquit themselves by simple denial. It was abolished by ordinance of the Black Prince in 1353 as being the "foster-mother of disorder"). (Public Record Office C53 162 m.11).

PUDDINGTON. *The foresters present that the draught beasts of Puddington had been driven to Chester Castle and there bailed until the next forest court, to answer for a stag found dead in the fields of the said township. The township came and because they could not find the evildoer, they were to pledge for amends of 6s. 8d. (33p), each man standing pledge for the other.*

THINGWALL, LANDICAN, BEBINGTON, LITTLE SAUGHALL and CLAUGHTON also had their draught beasts driven to Chester Castle as the same offence was committed in those townships. They were also bailed and pledged as above.

WALLASEY. *The foresters present that the dogs of Alexander Alan's son, Thomas Saughall, William Agnes's son, and Richard le Bagger killed a stag in the fields of Kirby-in-Wallasey. The township came and made a fine for 6s. 8d. Alexander and others did not come. It is witnessed that the Prior of Birkenhead stood bail for them, and he is dead. The sheriff was ordered to arrest them.*

SHOTWICK. *The foresters present that Hamo Baret wounded a stag in Shotwick wood and chased it with a dog over the River Dee. Hamo came.* (Nothing further follows).

There were also many 'Pleas of Vert' concerned with offences such as the building of houses in the forest, cutting down trees, digging marl pits and ploughing new fields. Several of these cases are listed below.

GREAT MOLLINGTON. *The foresters present that John Thorold cut down five oaks in 1276-7 in Great Mollington wood, of which he gave two to the Abbot of Chester and three to Sir Robert Lestrange and, in time, destroyed the whole wood with the help of Hamo and Adam, his tenants. When the foresters came to destrain him for the new ploughing, made to the forests great harm, he would not let justice be done but rebuffed them with force of arms, so that they raised the hue and cry.*

John came and could not deny the rebuff. He is adjudged to prison for contempt (pledges Adam Backford and Roger Pensby). As for the said oaks, he said that he had every right to cut them down for building or to give them to his neighbours for that purpose and that he gave no more nor did he make any other distruction. The sheriff is ordered to summon a jury. (Nothing further follows).

(The hue and cry was an ancient system of persuing a suspect whilst shouting and blowing a horn to attract the attention of neighbours and passers by who were bound by law to join in the chase). Today it would be similar to a "stop thief" situation.

WOODCHURCH. *Madoc Dut acted as pledge for William Legat to come to the next forest court to answer an accusation that he cut down eight oaks in Woodchurch wood. He is emerced (pledge, the sheriff).*

BEBINGTON. *Ranulf Launcelyne, accused of cutting down ten oaks in Bebington wood and selling them to the Abbot of Chester, came and acknowledged it. He was amerced (pledges William Launcelyne and James Poole).*

BEBINGTON. *The Warden of the Bebington House of Lepers assarted two acres of great oaks in Bebington, and took crops from them for two years. He also dug a ditch and planted a hedge there, which no wild beast could jump over. He came and acknowledged the assart, hedge and ditch, but said that he had every right to make them because of a grant made him by the king in these words:-*

(A transcript of letters of Edward I follows, which allow the warden to enclose five acres of waste within the metes of the forest with a small ditch and a low hedge, so that the king's beasts can go in and out, and to bring the five acres into cultivation. Date of letters: 6 September 1283).

It was adjudged that he should enjoy the assart, ditch and hedge, but the ditch and hedge were too big and ought to be remade so that the wild beasts can go in and out.

(An assart is land cleared of forest by grubbing up trees and bushes).

(The name leper hospital was abbreviated over the years and gave us the name Spital).

WILLASTON. *The township of Willaston dug 13 marl-pits, of which seven are dangerous. The men of Willaston came and could not deny it. They are amerced (pledges, each other). It was adjudged that seven of the pits could not be allowed, and must be filled in at the cost of the township.*

(Marl is a kind of limey clay which, for hundreds of years was dug up and scattered on the fields as fertiliser, in the days before railways could bring lime from the Pennines. Most of the ponds in Wirral were originally marl-pits).

NESS. *Philippa, Widow of Thomas Dutton, held five acres of land in Ness which Thomas Dutton 'assarted' in an alder grove, of which four acres were turned over to agriculture 16 years ago, and one acre eight years ago. She came and acknowledged it, and made a fine for the time being (pledges Hugh Dutton and Alexander Bamville).*

HESWALL. *Patrick Heswall ploughed up half an acre of land in Heswall, and took crops from it for four years. Patrick came and acknowledged it. He was amerced and made a fine for the meantime.*

TRANMERE. *William the Welshman and Richard Starky, Lords of Tranmere, held 7½ acres of land assarted from bramble and thorn there, of which two-thirds was cleared by William and one-third by John, Ranulf Starky's father (who is now dead). Crops were taken for six years. William came and acknowledged it. He was amerced and made a fine for the mean time (pledge Robert Starky). Richard came and acknowledged it. He was amerced and made a fine for the mean time (pledges Ranulf Starky and William son of Henry Tranmere).*

BIDSTON. *Cecily, Lady of Bidston, ploughed up 15 acres of land in Bidston, and took crops from them for four years, and she erected a house there since the last forest court. Cecily came and could not deny it. She was amerced (pledges Hamo Mascy and Ralph Vernon) and made a fine for the mean time (same pledges).*

Serious accusations concerning the cultivating of large amounts of Forest land were levelled at the clergy who as always seemed to have special rights recorded in old charters.

LANDICAN. *The Foresters present that Ralph Caldwell, Rector of Woodchurch, ploughed up eight acres in Landican, with the (? approval) of Ranulph Praers, Parson of Barthomley, to the great loss of the forest. Ranulph came and acknowledged it, but said that it had not harmed the forest. The regarders, asked about it, agreed with him. Therefore, he was acquitted.*

IRBY, WOODCHURCH, GREASBY, SUTTON, WHITBY, BROMBOROUGH, EASTHAM. *The Abbot of Chester ploughed up 20 acres of land in Irby, dug four marl-pits and assarted 1¼ acres of land in Woodchurch. In Greasby he ploughed 12 acres mowed two acres and assarted ½ an acre. In Sutton he ploughed up 45 acres, dug 42 marl-pits and enclosed eight acres of meadow between Sutton and Whitby. Each acre being worth about 4d (2p) a year.*

He also ploughed up 14 acres in Bromborough, enclosed two acres of waste where he built four houses and dug a marl pit. In Eastham he ploughed up 3½ acres and in Whitby five acres.

The Abbot was accused of harming the forest and of taking crops from these lands over a number of years. He acknowledged the assarts and ploughings, saying "he had every right to do so" pointing out that land in the Manors of Irby, Greasby, Sutton, Bromborough, Eastham and Whitby were confirmed to the Abbot and Convent by charters from the Earls of Chester.

The Abbot produced the charters, as well as a confirmation of King Edward I. The justicular replied that such "general words" relating to "the highest possible privilages" were not sufficient to disafforest the abbey lands. Judgement was given against the Abbot, but before execution it was referred to the King. It was also made known that no previous Abbot of Chester had ever been fined for assarts etc.

BIRKENHEAD. *The Prior of Birkenhead farmed 20 acres of land called Tollestowe* in Claughton which had been cleared of forest. A charter of Edward I proved that the priory owned the land. The Prior also enclosed land with ditches, dug a pond, built a piggery and blocked a highway from Birkenhead *to the hindrance of passers-by and to the harm of the forest. He said that he was well within his rights to do this, as can any free man who owns woodland. The regarders questioned about this agreed.*

Accounts of the court cases mentioned above, concern mainly tenants and under tenants of Norman origin, who were entrusted with running the estates of wealthy barons. The ditch digging and ploughing was largely done by serfs of Anglo-Saxon blood on their orders. Much of the land in their manors was waste and woodland. With the population growing, they wanted to build houses, plough and cultivate more land, but the Crown wanted Wirral to remain afforested.

The office of Master Forester passed to Alexander de Storeton and eventually to William Stanley of Storeton. The forest laws were often bent and flouted for personal gain. William Stanley allowed the people of certain villages to graze livestock in the forest when the deer were breeding and he was found guilty of this in court.

Storeton Hall, now part of a large farm, once the home of William Stanley, Master Forester.

The Gentry of Wirral were fed up with their crops being eaten by the beasts of the forest. They were also very frustrated at being held back from building, expanding their farms and making money from cultivating unused land. The foresters were probably regarded as 'secret police' spying on what the tenants were up to. These forest laws helped lead to Magna Carta.

At this time, church services in the forest parishes were suspended. This could have been due to the wooden churches being in need of maintenance work, which could not be done without cutting down trees for timber, and therefore breaking the law. Or possibly it was to stir people in high places into speaking out against the Forest Laws.

The people of Wirral petitioned Edward, Prince of Wales and Earl of Chester, known as the Black Prince (because he reputedly wore black armour). They asked him to disafforest their peninsula and free them from the yoke of the forest laws. Many of the knights and archers who had accompanied the Prince on his campaigns were from Wirral and he probably wanted them to remain loyal.

The Black Prince eventually declared Wirral disafforested, probably shortly before he died of sickness in June 1376. The disafforestation was confirmed by his father Edward III in July 1376 and witnessed by the Archbishop of Canterbury, John, King of Castille and ten other prominent people. But it was not confirmed by Parliament before Edward died a year later. In 1384 Richard II made the most of this and levied fines totalling 600 marks on the Wirral landowners, before the charter was confirmed in 1389.

When Wirral had been declared disafforested, William Stanley claimed for loss of fees and his office as Master Forester. It was ruled that the Black Prince had not wanted Stanley to suffer financially due to disafforestation and in 1397 he was granted a yearly compensational payment of 20 marks which was to be passed on to his son.

After Wirral as a whole was disafforested, five deer parks enclosed by walls and fences were maintained in Bidston, Hooton, Shotwick, Puddington and Neston. Parts of a wall built by John Stanley enclosing a 160 acre deer park on Bidston Hill are still standing and the gateway into Neston deer park gave us the name Parkgate.

Bidston Hill, once a deer park.

People today probably find it difficult to imagine the importance of hunting to those of previous centuries. With no proper shops, refrigerators or tinned food, fresh meat was a necessity. There was little or no organised entertainment and hunting provided food and fun. Also, an invitation to hunt often resulted in business being done, as perhaps it is today over a game of golf. Skilful riding and hunting prowess was admired, just as today, a mans boxing, rugby or footballing ability might be.

Hunting was also a kind of training for war, which was part of peoples lives in the Middle Ages. Stalking game, riding down a wild boar or wolf with spear or lance and shooting deer with bow-and-arrows were all skills called upon in battle. A skilful fearless hunter usually turned out to be a good warrior.

The ancient woods of Wirral have nearly all gone. Apart from Bidston Hill, much of the woodland we see in Wirral today was planted by landowners in the last century. However, small pockets of woodland which were not considered worth the effort to clear still survive in little rough dales here and there. Some of these being *Harrock Wood* in Irby, *The Dungeon* at Thurstaston, *Barnston Dale* and *Lower Heath Wood* on the borders of Thingwall, Barnston and Storeton, which are my "neck of the woods".

Lower Heath Wood, one of a number of wooded dales which has not changed for centuries and where wild deer once roamed. This view is from the public footpath leading to Storeton from Lower Thingwall Lane.

WIRRAL COUNTRY WOMEN AT WORK

During the last century agriculture was by far the largest source of employment in Wirral. In 1811 there were only 11,579 people living in Wirral and out of the 2,265 old enough to work, 1,468 were engaged in agriculture. During the reign of Queen Victoria, (1837 - 1901) the Mersey bank of Wirral had industrialised rapidly; factories, flour mills, docks and shipyards etc. had sprung up providing employment for many thousands of people, but in the rest of Wirral farms still provided employment for a very large proportion of workers.

Just as many women do today, Victorian women worked. Single women and widows often worked full time as cooks and maids etc. "living-in" at the houses of the well-to-do, or as general servants on farms large and small.

Married women with children were home-makers first and foremost and they certainly had their hands full, washing by hand and cooking on open fires etc. Most working class families were large and badly off in those days. Any chance to add a few pence to the family budget was grabbed with both hands. If part time or casual jobs came along, women would try to fit them in and work round their family tasks. Working women did not earn anywhere near as much as men, usually half the going rate.

In rural Wirral there were not many employment options open to women to enable them to add to their housekeeping. Most married women who worked were employed in agriculture, others took in washing and a few, living in villages close to the sea or River Dee gathered shellfish on the beach.

A large number of women were registered as laundresses and washerwomen. Washing and ironing for the well off, or for men living alone or in lodgings, provided some women with a regular income. They were able to do the washing in their own homes and work flexible hours which was important. But in most small villages the scope was limited as there were often more women willing to take in washing than people to wash for. To make a reasonable amount of money, women might have to walk to areas like Oxton, Prenton, West Kirby or Heswall where there would be a number of well off families who would pay to have their washing done.

A few women were recorded as 'mangle keepers', they either mangled peoples washing for them or people paid to use the mangle. One such 'mangle keeper' recorded living in Leighton Road, Neston in 1851 was 50 year old Mary Hughes; another was Susannah Roberts, a Cornish born 41 year old widow from Hoose Village.

Gathering shellfish along the Dee at low tide gave women from the riverside villages the prospect of earning a bit of money daily. There were a number of women registered as cockle gatherers or cockle getters. In 1851 two Ness cockle gatherers were Manchester-born Bridget Ellison aged 46 of *New Houses* and Margaret Littlemore aged 65 of the *Colliery*. Margaret's 68 year old husband Joseph had been a coal miner but was then registered as a pauper; they were obviously finding it hard to make ends meet. With no state benefits the only help people might expect in those days was from family or the church. It was very much a case of work or want.

There were farms in all villages which, with their animals and varied crops, gave women employment, off and on through the year. When there was no casual work to be done these country women picked hazel nuts, blackberries and mushrooms, baked pies and made jam. A few women gathered tufts of sheep's wool stuck stuck to the briers. These were built up and spun into yarn for knitting socks and darning clothes.

They also gathered fire wood to store away for the winter. Although coal was cheap it still cost money and logs were free. I have spent many a day gathering logs myself. Hawthorn, oak, beech, ash and birch are among the best burning woods as they do not spit. Ash was particularly sought after as it splits easily and, unlike other woods, it burns well without being seasoned. Hawthorn burns fiercely and when hedges were cut the branches were put to one side. Silver birch was plentiful as it grew well on the rough heath land; it seasons quickly and the bark burns like paper.

Dead sticks were broken from the hedges and stored in a dry place for kindling. Big branches were carried home for the menfolk to saw up. Sometimes women and their bigger children looked for dead branches higher up the trees and threw ropes over them and snapped them off. If a dead tree blew down on a road or common it was not long before the locals cleared it. It was a 'windfall' for them. At harvest home a farmer might give a couple of fallen or dead trees to his workers as an extra bit of a thank you, to help them through the winter. The way of life in those days was "waste not, want not".

People used to say the logs warmed them twice, once cutting them and then again at night burning them. They reckoned that three bags of logs lasted about as long as one bag of coal. My dad says the old log fire was more healthy than central heating and you could spit on it.

Apart from their traditional jobs such as dairy maids, farmers were quite happy to employ women to do any work they were capable of doing equal to men, as they worked for less money.

Jobs which they could stop and start as they pleased were the most convenient to mothers with children at school. If there was no older relation available to look after her younger children, a mother would often take them to the fields with her. In the warmer months young women took their new babies with them and laid them in baskets near by, taking time out to breast feed them when necessary.

Whatever the task the small gangs of women usually sang as they worked, sometimes together or sometimes one would sing a song and the others joined in at the chorus. At break times they drank jugs of tea whilst men were given ale.

There was once a large amount of common and waste land in Wirral on which local people had the ancient right to graze livestock, gather firewood and quarry stone etc. During the last century much of this land was enclosed by the Crown and sold off as farm land. Between 1800 and 1850 there were 35 enclosures acts passed by Parliament concerning Cheshire. Villages all over Wirral were robbed of their common land, some more than others, such as Wallasey and West Kirby where 816 acres were enclosed.

The 1849 tithe map of Heswall and Gayton numbers 111 small fields and crofts recorded as 'enclosures'. After 1850 another 12 acts were passed causing among others, the enclosure of 205 acres at Thurstaston, to the outrage of the village communities.

This enclosed land was cleared of thorn, briars, gorse and birch etc. for cultivation. When many of these new fields were ploughed for the first time, a large number of stones were brought up. The new fields had to be picked clear of stones to save the farm implements from damage and to improve the land. Stone picking was a job given to women and children.

Sometimes the stones were gathered in horse buckets and the women were paid by the bucket, but in fields which were very stony, sticks were knocked in the ground every 10 yards, in rows 10 yards apart. Then the women, assisted by their children, cleared one patch at a time by throwing the stones a maximum of 15 feet to the nearest stick. When each 10 yard patch was cleared they moved on from stick to stick.

When all the stones had been thrown in rucks, farm labourers would come to the field and load them onto horse drawn carts. The women were paid so much per cart load. Large stones were obviously loaded one at a time, but little'ns were shovelled up and thrown on. Large lumps of sandstone were off loaded at the farm-yard and kept for repairing buildings and walls. Granite duck stones were used to cobble the yards. Some smaller stones were used to pack round gate posts to make them solid, most were dumped in pot holes or used to level the rough lanes, cart tracks and paths, to provide man and beast with a more solid footing.

There were no mechanical muck spreaders in Victorian days so spreading manure was done with a fork. During the winter muck was carted from stables, cattle sheds, shippens and farm middens to the fields for spreading, before being ploughed under to feed the next years crops. Horses pulled the loaded carts across the fields when the ground was hard with frost so that the narrow wooden wheels did not sink. The farmer walked behind the cart and raked a pile of muck off the back every six yards in rows six yards apart ready for spreading with forks to evenly fertilise the field. Muck spreading or "knocking muck about" as it was often referred to was another job often done by women.

Loading muck at Storeton Hall Farm during the Great War.
Left to right; Ralph Wright, ? Ashcroft, Martin ?, George Wright.

In spring and through the summer when weeds grew rapidly among the potato, mangold and turnip crops etc, women and children were employed to weed. Male farm workers were used for heavier and more skilled work.

During the warm summer months, when hay making time came round, some village women were often hired to rake the scythed hay into rows after it had dried out in the sun. Other women followed and carefully built the rows of hay into small domed stacks called hay cocks, ready for carting and so that the rain would run off if the weather changed. These cocks were not made too high so that the men could load them onto the hay wagon in one lift with a pikle or pitch fork, as they are called in other parts of the country.

Farmers wives 'knocking muck about' in Storeton fields during the Great War.
Left to right; Mrs. Hughes, Mrs. Wright, Mrs. Roxburgh, Mrs. Taylor and Mrs. Ollerhead.

The next big job on the farm calendar after hay making was the corn harvest at the end of summer. Men scythed the corn and women came behind, gathered it up and tied it in sheaves with straw bands. The sheaves were then built into stooks. Stooks were small stacks made from about eight sheaves. They were stood up so as to let the wind blow through and dry them while they stood waiting to be carted to the corn stack.

By the turn of the century the demand for female labour on farms fell dramatically due to mechanisation. Farm machinery such as horse-drawn mowing machines for cutting hay and self-binders which cut the corn and bound it in sheaves, were used all over Wirral. The temporary women farm workers suffered a double blow from mechanisation. Not only was much of their traditional work at harvest time lost, but men who used to scythe the crops were put to alternative work and there were always plenty of temporary Irish labourers.

At Christmas time plucking and dressing poultry might give some women a few days' employment but the amount of farm work was very limited. The days of farm work being a major employer of females was well and truly over except for the wives and daughters of smallholders. Women had to look to indoor employment. Wirral's villages were growing rapidly, due mainly to the railway network, and big houses, shops and hospitals were being built, all providing work for women, many of whom once relied on farm work. There were no nurseries or old people's homes as such in those days and girls were often employed as nursemaids and companions to old ladies.

During the Great War, waste and unused land was cleared and cultivated as food was in short supply. I know one old man who, with other local lads and women stone picked a newly ploughed field in 1916. He was paid a penny a bucket. In those days he would have had to pick 240 buckets of stones (40 a day for a six day week) to earn £1.

Milking was still done by hand and dairy maids milked as fast as men, a few women could handle horses as good as men. This is recorded at a ploughing match at Mr. T.E. Johnsons farm at Ness in 1917 where ladies ploughed using teams of horses belonging to or 'with' Wirral farmers.

Ladies Open Class;   1. Margaret Foster, with F. A. Dutton, Ness.
2. Maud Stamford, with John Johnson, Burton.
3. Mrs. Marks, with R. Leech, Willaston.

Team Of Horses Ploughing Proper Depth And Appointed Quantity Of Land.
1. A. Hamilton, with W. Allen, Leighton.
2. Mrs. Marks, with R. Leech, Willaston.
3. Ruth Peake, with R. Jones, Shotwick Lodge.
4. J. Crabb, with R. Leech, Willaston.
   Res., W. Moore, with Mrs. Dodd, Mill Hill, Irby.
   H.C., J. Millington, with J. Mealor, Little Neston.

Years ago potatoes were dug by men with forks. Before the Second World War the horse drawn spinner was invented which was pulled up and down the rows, lifting and kicking the potatoes out onto the open ground ready for picking up. This made harvesting potatoes a lighter job (although back breaking after a while) and more suitable for women than the old method of digging.

Farms across Wirral employed gangs of women for potato picking. They gathered them in baskets or buckets and tipped them into sacks or hampers. Payment was either by the day or by how many hampers or sacks they filled. Sometimes the potatoes went straight out of the fields on carts to shops or markets.

Often they were hogged as we say in Wirral, in other areas people say clamped. When large amounts of potatoes, turnips, beetroot or mangolds were harvested they were usually hogged in the fields as there was not the storage space for them in the farm buildings. To make a hog, first of all a dry patch of the field was chosen, preferably on slightly higher ground and close to the lane or gate. The cart loads of potatoes were tipped on the chosen spot to form a big oblong mound. The potatoes were covered with a layer of straw, then a trench was dug round them and the soil was spread on top of the straw. This kept the frost out and the trench helped drainage. Every few yards a pottery drain pipe was inserted in the hog for ventilation and plugged with a wad of straw to keep the frost out. In olden days the potato plant tops were thrown on top of the hog for good measure.

Once or twice a week through the winter months the hogs were opened up and potatoes were riddled and bagged in three different sizes, shop size, sets and chats. On some farms women did this. On very cold winter days they lit a small fire by the hog, burning bits of wood and potato tops while they worked. The shop size potatoes were sold by the hundredweight and sets, which were the size of hen eggs, were kept back for next years seed. The little'ns called 'chats' were fed to the pigs, but in the olden days some of the poorer people would buy sacks of chats to make cheap meals. Most were too small to peel so they were washed and boiled in their jackets.

Farmers with large potato crops had regular customers such as chip shops, schools or hospitals. When the Bowden family ran *Home Farm* at Woodchurch for James Ball, they grew up to 90 acres of potatoes and supplied St. Catherine's Hospital with three tons a week.

During the Great War so many men left the farms to join the army that farmers struggled to harvest crops at a time when the country was desperately short of food due to German submarines sinking so much of our shipping. In 1917 Mr. R. Potheroe minister of agriculture formed a Womens Land Army, recruited and run by Dame Muriel Talbot. By 1918 there were over 23,000 women in the land army serving on farms and market gardens all over Britain; many were recruited from towns. They were paid 18 shillings (90p) per week. Another measure to relieve the shortage of labour in agriculture was to allow boys of 12 and 13 to leave school.

Also to help the war effort, the Women's Institute was formed in 1917 in villages across Britain. Women were given talks on how to be more efficient in the home with their rations and what little they had. Gardening, cooking and craft tips were passed on in talks and demonstrations. The women organised village jumble sales, plays etc. and were encouraged to help their neighbours more. All this was very important for the morale of our women who came from all classes and walks of life and who had suffered years of worry, bad news and hardship.

When the Second World War started in 1939 our women were more organised. The Land Army was re-formed a couple of months before war was declared. About 1,000 young ladies were trained and registered on the books, available to go to farms which might be short handed if and when the war started. By the end of 1939 2,800 girls had enlisted and during 1941 about 1,000 girls a month were signing up. As in any organisation a number of girls chucked it, but most stuck it out and "soldiered on".

The Land Girls were employed not only by farmers but by market gardeners and the forestry commission. There were many thousands of girls in the organisation and they were employed all over Britain at all kinds of agricultural work, from weeding turnips and looking after poultry to loading hay and helping with the thrashing machine at harvest time. At Frodsham, just outside Wirral, Land Girls helped with the heavy task of draining the marshes for grazing.

These patriotic young ladies certainly helped to win the war, not only by releasing farm workers for military service, but by their enthusiasm and sheer hard work, for a wage of only 48 shillings (£2.40)a week. Many girls had loved ones serving in our armed forces and they wanted to "do their bit". There was also a type of "flying squad" of girls, over 26,000 of them, who volunteered to be sent anywhere where there was a desperate short-term need of farm labour. These girls saved the day many times, particularly at harvest. They might sleep in one of the hundreds of Land Army Hostels, a homely cottage or an old country mansion. Lady Denman, the Honorary Director of the Land Army, of Belcombe Place in Sussex, allowed her home to be used as the headquarters. She also allowed her tennis courts to be used for livestock grazing.

The Women's Institutes and Mothers' Union also continued with their very useful role during the Second World War.

In both World Wars many of these young women married men they met on the farms. One such girl was Rose Waller of West Kirby, who, in 1917, along with her sister May, worked at *Lower Farm,* Prenton, now the *Saddle Club*. The farm was managed by Edwin Purdie for his widowed aunt Mrs. Sally Johnson. May eventually joined the Womens Army Corps and served in France but Rose stayed on at the farm as she had fallen in love with Edwin who she later married. Eventually Mr. and Mrs. Purdie took the tenancy of *New Home Farm* in Holm Lane, Oxton, the farm passed to their son Eddy an old friend of mine who fought in North Africa and Italy in Second World War. After the farm and its land in the *Flat Lanes* were built on during the 1960s and '70s, Eddy farmed at *Mill Hill Farm,* Irby until he died a few years ago after taking bad whilst driving back from Chester cattle market. Eddy is survived by his son Mark and sister Mrs. Doris Evetts of Irby.

Today very few women are employed on Wirral's farms as there is no work for them. Gangs of women picked potatoes on Wirral's farms through the 1950s, but in the 1960s better paid work became available such as in Cadbury's factory and Champion Spark Plugs etc. and women potato pickers largely became a thing of the past.

Women 'tater pickers in the 1960s enjoying a well earned cup of tea. Also pictured with the ladies in Landican fields is ploughman Alf Oxton. This year (1996) Alf is in his 50th year of employment at Home Farm, Landican. In the background is the Woodchurch Estate where most of the women lived.

Farms which employed six men and maybe a dairy-maid in Victorian times can now be worked by the tenant and one man using modern machinery.

Wirral's Victorian country women had extremely hard lives. Many, such as my grandmother, gave birth to more than a dozen children at home with no proper medical back-up. Things which are simple for us today such as boiling a pot of water took time and effort as there was no running water or electricity. The water would have to be drawn out of a well, then a fire lit and stoked up. Even after working in the fields wives had to cook, wash clothes, clean, mend etc. as well as be mothers and nurses. But they got on with life and were usually very cheerful by all accounts.

Families were close and a visit from a relation or friend was looked forward to whereas today visitors are often seen as an interruption to the night's television viewing. Farm labourers and smallholders worked hard seven days a week in all weathers for low wages, but with a happy family life and a good mother or wife behind them they could face the hardships. As the old saying goes "behind every good man is a better woman".

THE NEW CUT TO CHESTER

It is common knowledge that Chester was one of the most important Roman cities in Britain. It was a port and also a garrison town, home of the 20th Roman Legion. On the high ground protected by a curve in the river, they built the fort called Deva. The Romans also had an outpost and naval base at the small port of Great Meols in Wirral.

In Anglo-Saxon times Chester was a very wealthy and busy port. It had its own mint and its wealth attracted an invasion by the Danes in 893 and a Viking fleet from the Isle of Man in 980.

The importance of Chester was shown when, in 973, King Edgar visited the city where eight kings and sub-kings came to pay him tribute. They rowed him down the Dee and through the city, four each side. The kings were Kenneth III of Scotland, Howell of North Wales, Owen of South Wales, Macon of the Isle of Man, Malcolm of Cumberland, James of Galloway, and two joint rulers, Sfreth, of South Wales and Inkil of Cumberland.

In the Domesday Book it is recorded that before 1066, in the City of Chester, there were 431 houses paying tax and as well as these the Bishop had a further 56 houses paying tax. There were seven moneyers in the City. Moneyers were men who were licensed to make coins. The government provided them with dies to make the coins and they were allowed to keep six silver pennies in the pound.

(The silver penny had been introduced in 735 by King Offa. In 800 Charlemagne, King of the Franks and Holy Roman Emperor, ordered 240 denarii or silver pennies to be made from one pound weight of silver. This monetary system was adopted in England and until 1971 there were 240 pence to the pound).

The Chester moneyers used silver from local Welsh lead mines. Silver is found in lead ores and although the mines were actually lead mines a lot of silver was produced even in Roman times. The importing of martens' skins is also mentioned in the Domesday Book as being an important trade.

In Norman times also, Chester was an extremely important port and military base. Ships sailed to and from Ireland, France, Spain and Germany, and troops gathered there for Welsh and Irish campaigns.

During the Middle Ages the world climate grew colder and the sea level dropped. The River Dee in the Chester area began to silt up due to shifting sands and erosion of the shoreline. Also in Norman times a weir had been built at Chester which restricted the flow of the river. Eventually the water was only deep enough to allow small boats to reach the Roodee.

Ships began to use the smaller Wirral ports to load and off-load cargo which, along with passengers, had to be transported to Chester on smaller boats or by road. These small Wirral ports were all referred to as the Port of Chester in shipping terms as they were under its jurisdiction.

Shotwick, being one of the nearest anchorages to Chester, became a busy port and during the reign of Henry VI (1422-71) a quay was built there. The sand eventually reduced the depth of the channel at Shotwick and shipping moved further up the coast into the deeper water at Burton Point and Denhall. Burton Church is dedicated to St. Nicholas, the patron saint of mariners and at Denhall was the ancient Hospital of St. Andrew for the poor, and shipwrecked mariners. This indicates that there was a great deal of shipping using the lower Wirral ports during the Middle Ages.

In 1541 the merchants of Chester started collecting money to build a new quay at *Lyghtfote Pole* (Lightfoots Pool) at Little Neston. Work began on the *New Haven* (later called the New Quay) in 1569 and it served as a port for about 200 years. Not only passengers and goods but Irish cattle and Welsh ponies were shipped into Neston. Also army horses and troops were marched out from Chester to Neston for shipment to Ireland.

All ports in Wirral and on the Welsh side of the Dee and round the coast as far as Rhyl, were part of the Port of Chester. In 1569, even Liverpool was still 'a creek within the Port of Chester', in legal terms, with a fleet of only 12 ships. Over half a century later, during the reign of Charles I (1625-49) £100 ship money was demanded from Chester but only £15 from Liverpool.

In Captain Grenville Collins' lifetime the River Dee was still the most important river, with the Mersey playing second fiddle. In 1687 when Liverpool was beginning to rival Chester, he wrote; .."*at Nesson and Dorpool, lower down than Chester, where you may anchor in three-fathom water*" (18 feet). Gayton, Dawpool, Caldy, West Kirby, Hilbre Island and Hoylake, all played an important part in shipping both passengers and cargo.

In 1699 an attempt was made to improve the channel from Neston to Chester. Whatever improvement there was did not last long as more schemes were put forward to improve navigation to Chester. The main problem was that the River Dee had such a wide estuary that the tidal flow did not scour the channel.

The New Quay (by this time called the Old Quay) in Little Neston was in decline as it became too shallow for the larger ships. Parkgate, already a port, a little higher up the river, took over as the most important on the Dee with ferry services to Dublin, Flint and Bagillt. Dawpool near Thurstaston also ran an Irish ferry service to Ringsend.

The New Cut looking toward Chester from the Queensferry Bridge.

Deep sea vessels bound for Chester were firstly anchored in the Hoyle Lake for quarantine before proceeding to Parkgate or elsewhere. At Parkgate, cargoes were transfered from ships to smaller craft and taken ashore or to Chester. Only small boats could still reach Chester and it was obvious that unless something was done, eventually the River Dee would no longer be navigable and Chester would die as a port.

In 1731 Nathaniel Kinderley of Lincolnshire suggested that a deep-water channel could be cut from Chester to deeper waters near Flint. There was opposition to the scheme from the Port of Liverpool which would obviously suffer if Chester once again became a deep-sea port. After an act of Parliament was passed, a wide channel, to be 16 feet deep at high tide, was dug along the Welsh coast and through the *White Sands* during 1735-6. This *New Cut* was not the natural course of the river, as the deep water channel flowed to Chester along the Wirral coast.

Lower down the Dee, people could no longer ford the river by wading across as they had done for centuries because the New Cut was far too deep, so ferry services were laid on from Saltney and Queensferry.

The New Cut was a success, giving Chester a new lease of life. Docking facilities were built along the Cut at Chester, Saltney, Sandycroft, Queensferry and Connah's Quay (believed to be named after an Irish merchant). The River Dee Company was formed in 1740 to maintain the depth of the New Cut and keep it navigable. Parkgate remained a very important port particularly for Irish shipping, due mainly to its ferry and mail-boat service which ran to Dublin four times a week.

Even with the New Cut, Chester could not now compete with Liverpool whose sea trade was growing in leaps and bounds. One great draw-back for Chester was that the larger vessels needed two tides to reach the city. On one tide the ship could sail from the open sea to Flint, but by then the tide had turned and it was too shallow to continue up the Cut to Chester. The ships had to anchor and await the next tide to sail the remaining 13 miles into the city.

Hundreds of coasters a year sailed the New Cut in the late 1700s, on their way to and from Liverpool, London, Bristol, Scotland and ports along the Welsh coast, particularly Caernarvon, Beaumaris and Conwy. Deep sea ships sailed mainly to and from Ireland but a few traded with various European countries including Russia and one or two sailed to Africa, Jamaica and Newfoundland.

The New Cut enabled Chester to play a small part in the slave trade which was dominated by Bristol, London and Liverpool, although even Lancaster, Preston and Poulton-le-Fylde were involved. During the 1750s a few Chester ships made voyages to Africa with knives, guns, cloth, rum and beads for bartering to tribal chiefs for slaves. The African slaves were then transported to the West Indies and America where they were sold or bartered for sugar, coffee, tobacco, rum and cotton etc. These luxury goods were brought back to Chester and sold at great profit.

In 1757 the Chester slave ship *Black Prince* and two Liverpool ships, the *Ogden* and the *Penelope* were attacked by two heavily armed French men-of-war at Malimba on the West African coast. The slave ships engaged the French vessels but were heavily out gunned. Rather than surrender, the three English captains ran their ships ashore. A French boarding party made for the *Black Prince* but the Chester men fought them off and escaped. The next day French sailors burnt her and allowed about 70 natives to plunder the *Ogden* after laying a fuse to the powder magazine. Then they deliberately blew the Liverpool ship up killing all the Africans on board. Captain William Creevey of the *Black Prince* eventually made his way home via Rotterdam.

The odd slave must have been transported down the Dee to work in a few houses of the wealthy. Neston Church records indicate that at least one or two slaves lived in that village.

The following burial recorded at Neston is almost certainly that of a slave; *1802, Christian Modesty, said to be very old.* Also the following baptism, probably of a former slave; *1810, Thomas, a boy from the coast of Africa, servant to Mr. Nicolas Aspinall.* Another link with slavery and privateering was the Parkgate pilot of the early 1800s, Fortunatus Wright, probably a grandson of the famous privateer ship's captain of the same name.

In 1817, a company called the River Dee Company, which had been formed to keep the channel to Chester navigable, was forced to engage the famous engineer Thomas Telford to improve the New Cut, as it had begun to silt up. Telford was also consulted in 1822 about a proposed scheme to run a steam packet service from Dawpool to Dublin. The cost was estimated at £30,000, a considerable sum in those days and the idea was scrapped.

Digging the New Cut greatly speeded up the silting of the Wirral coast. Changing the course of the river caused the tide to deposit a great amount of silt between the South Wirral shore and the New Cut, creating an ever spreading marsh. By 1810 the channel at Parkgate was very seriously silted. The water was no longer deep enough for large vessels and the Parkgate to Dublin mail-boat service was forced to transfer to Liverpool. In 1837 there was a proposal to cut a canal from Heswall to Chester but this idea also came to nothing.

Small cargo and fishing boats had for centuries been built on the shores of the Dee in every village, and the odd deep sea ship was built on the shore; one such vessel was built at Dawpool in 1699. The deeper waters of the New Cut now made it possible to build fairly large ships on the Dee. There were only three shipyards on the river in the late 1700s, two were in Chester and one operated in Parkgate for a few years. They used mostly Cheshire and Welsh timber, building various vessels including ships, brigantines, sloops, galliots and flats.

By the mid 1800s there were more than a dozen shipyards on the Dee, nearly all from Flint down to Chester, with one each in Talacre, Mostyn, and Bagillt, from John Dawson's yard in Talacre, to the yard of Cox & Miller in Chester. Hundreds of ships were built for both coastal trade and deep sea. Some were only about 12 tons but many were up to 500 tons and some a lot bigger. All kinds of vessels were built including fishing boats, schooners and Royal Naval brigs. In 1806 more ships were built on the River Dee than on the Mersey.

The most famous and tragic ship built on the River Dee was the 2,719 ton *Royal Charter* built at the Sandycroft yard of George Cramm in 1855. The New Cut was too narrow for this 336 feet long ship to be launched in the normal way, so she went down the slip sideways, with great difficulty. Soon after launch she ran aground off Flint and was badly damaged, suffering among other things, a bent keel. After major repairs in Liverpool, the 'Royal Charter' was used on the Australia run, carrying cargo and passengers.

In 1859 whilst returning to Liverpool from Melbourne, she was caught in a force 12 gale or rather a hurricane, off Anglesey. It was the worst storm ever recorded by the Liverpool Observatory. The passengers aboard the *Royal Charter* were mostly miners and their families returning to England after making their fortune in the Australian gold rush. The ship was carrying £370,000 in gold bars and sovereigns, plus an unknown amount which the passengers had on their person in money belts and bags, etc.

She broke in two off Moelfre on the coast of Anglesey and out of about 500 men, women and children, only about 40 men survived, mainly due to local villagers dragging them from the rocks. All ships officers, women and children were lost, most were dashed against rocks by the mountainous seas. Many men went straight under due to their heavy money belts and the thick clothing they wore in those days. The women in particular had no chance of swimming, being dressed in long frocks and petticoats.

One of the dead was young crewman Isaac Lewis of Moelfre village who was said to have made it ashore, only to be swept from the rocks after nearly reaching his father, and calling to him "Oh Father, I have come home to be drowned".

The next day the storm was over and some villagers noticed gold coins and other valuables in the rocks. The word spread and people came from near and far to comb the beaches so that Marines and Militia were sent to guard the wreck and prevent people from robbing corpses. Eventually most of the cargo of gold was recovered. But no one will ever know how much gold was carried by the passengers or how many beach-combers made fortunes.

The River Dee Company came to possess thousands of acres of marshes reclaimed from the sea at Sealand, Sandycroft, Shotton, Saughall and Shotwick. The company received thousands of pounds a year in rent for these lands and it appeared it was more concerned in recovering and leasing the marshland than keeping the New Cut to the required depth for shipping. This resulted in the responsibility of the maintenance and upkeep of the New Cut being taken out of the hands of the River Dee Company and given to the Dee Conservancy Board in 1889.

As the old saying goes "every cloud has a silver lining", and this was true of the Dee Estuary. Although the silting of the river was putting Wirral men out of work, the opportunity to buy cheap marshland for factory building attracted Harry and James Summers, nailmakers of Stalybridge, to the area. In 1895 they bought 40 acres of marshland at Harwarden bridge close to the Birkenhead and Chester railway line and built an ironworks. Eventually they expanded and bought 10,000 acres at five shillings (25p) an acre and in the works heyday employed 13,000 men, many of them from Wirral and Chester.

Due to continual silting of the Dee, which made it difficult and time consuming to reach Chester, the Welsh ports along the New Cut became more important. With the coming of the railway, coal and bricks could be transported directly by train from Buckley colliery and brickworks to the Connah's Quay for shipment, mainly to Ireland and Liverpool.

The list below records six days' shipping, from 14th to 19th of October 1910 and shows how the Welsh ports on the New Cut had taken over from Chester, but by this time even these ports were in decline.

IMPORTS.

DATE	NAME OF SHIP	FROM	TO	CARGO
Oct. 14	Catherine Latham	Dublin	Flint	Scrap Iron.
Oct. 16	Penrhyn S.S.	Liverpool	Flint	Wheat
Oct. 16	The Star	Liverpool	Flint	Wheat
Oct. 16	Glittering Star	Liverpool	Harwarden Bridge	Spelter
Oct. 16	Ellen	Liverpool	Harwarden Bridge	Spelter
Oct. 16	Agness Glover	Belfast	Chester	Grass Seed
Oct. 17	Lizzie	Fowey	Flint	China Clay
Oct. 17	Florence Louise	Southhampton	Harwarden Bridge	Loam
Oct. 18	Sarah Ann Widdup	Glasgow	Harwarden Bridge	Bricks
Oct. 18	Petrel	Liverpool	Saltney	Grain
Oct. 18	Edward Blower	Liverpool	Saltney	Grain
Oct. 18	Maggie S.S.	Liverpool	Saltney	Grain
Oct. 18	Assurance S.S.	Penmaenmawr	Chester	Stone

EXPORTS.

Oct. 17	Vriendschap	Queensferry	Randers (Denmark)	Creosote Oil
Oct. 18	Thomas & Anne	Flint	Liverpool	Salt Cake
Oct. 18	Victoria	Flint	Liverpool	Chemicals
Oct. 18	Despatch	Connah's Qu.	Belfast	Bricks
Oct. 18	Glad Tidings	Connah's Qu.	Cork	Bricks
Oct. 18	Not Forgot	Connah's Qu.	Liverpool	Bricks
Oct. 18	Mourne S.S.	Queensferry	Swansea	CoalTar Pitch
Oct. 19	Eller S.S.	Queensferry	Swansea	CoalTar Pitch

By the time of the Great War (1914-18), in which several Chester ships were sunk, trade and shipbuilding on the Dee were well in decline and only a few shipyards were still operating. However a fleet of over 20 coasters of between 100 and 200 tons was operating regularly from Summers Steelworks during the 1920s and 1930s. They were used to ship in pig iron from Cumberland and to export slag and ash to Ireland and Scotland to be used as fertilizer.

During the 1930s J.Crichton & Co. were still building ships at Connah's Quay and Saltney, whilst Abdela & Mitchell were still building at Queensferry. These three yards closed before the Second World War. There were still a few coasters sailing from Connahs Quay and Summers Steel Works after the Second World War, but by the 1950s, shipping along the New Cut was more or less finished. The last locally owned ships belonged to Coppack's, the old shipowning family from Connah's Quay.

For many years now the New Cut has been too shallow to allow ships to reach Chester, Connah's Quay, Queensferry etc. and the ports have died. Mostyn, near the mouth of the Dee is still quite a busy little port and on very high tides small ships can still get down to Shotton Steel Works. Most of the steel exported from Shotton is shipped from Mostyn and Liverpool but the works' jetty is still available and periodically used. Gordon Smith of British Steel tells me that in 1995 a ship came to Shotton Steel Works jetty at high tide on the 5th of December, loaded 1500 tons of finished steel product and sailed for France at high tide the following day. The new motorway bridge across the Dee at Shotton will be high enough to allow ships to sail under to the Steel Works' Jetty.

Ships sailing from Chester and its smaller Deeside ports in Wales and Wirral had for hundreds of years employed quite a number of local men as crew. Not all seafarers lived in the ports themselves. During the 1700s, nearly every Wirral village, at one time or another, had one or two men recorded as mariners in church records. Two of my own ancestors' occupations are recorded as mariners, John Dawson of Thurstaston who married Susan Smoult at Childwall in 1703 and Simon Dawson of Irby who died in 1725. Villages around Chester and in Wales also had their fair share of mariners. Sadly today, the Dee no longer has large numbers of local seafarers sailing its waters.

As regards being a port, Chester is now back to square one. In digging the New Cut and trying to make the City a port again, Wirral was robbed of the natural channel which gave life to the small ports and fishing villages along our coast. Less than 100 years after the New Cut was dug, no laden ship could come anywhere near the quay wall at Parkgate, due to the formation of a large sand bank. Even far away Hoylake was put out of business. In 1700 the Hoyle Lake was ½ mile wide, 15 feet deep at one end and 30 feet deep at the other when the tide was out. Due to changing tidal flows caused by the New Cut, by 1844 the lake was only two foot deep at one end and dry at the other. Today there is no Hoyle Lake at all, just sand banks

Changing the course of the river caused the silt washed down Gayton Gutter and along the Parkgate / Neston channel to be deposited at Sealand where the old channel was blocked from flowing into the New Cut. This created an ever spreading marsh which in my father's lifetime alone has spread from Neston to Thurstaston.

In 1086 both Blacon and Saughall had fisheries, but today both these places are miles from the sea. Only the name of *Blacon Point* and old farms and houses in the Saughall area, such as *Seahill Farm* and *Wash Hall* (built near wash of the tide), bear witness to their past links with the sea.

Today, R.A.F. Sealand, Deeside Industrial Park, Shotton Steel Works, Shotton Paper Mills etc. and housing estates such as Garden City (built by John Summers for steelworkers) stand where 200 - 250 years ago sea water flowed. Livestock graze, crops grow and farms stand where ships once sailed and fish swam. The very name Sealand, means land re-claimed from the sea.

Burton Point where ships once tied up.

The Dee marshes from Burton Point looking toward Neston.
These cliffs were once washed by the tide twice a day.

A glance at a map, or the River Dee whilst driving over the Queensferry bridge, and the straight course of the New Cut can be seen. Since ancient times the River Dee had marked the border between North Wales and England. Because of the New Cut, thousands of acres of Wales are now on the English side of the river.

A number of pleasant Wirral villages have lost their beaches, but many of their inhabitants have found work in industrial sites built on the marsh. The marsh is still spreading. Let's hope it never reaches Hilbre and we don't lose Wirral's only islands.

THE DEE FISHERMEN

For centuries villagers in the Neston area have been fishermen, both part- and full-time. Neston was the most populous parish in Wirral until the 1830s when it was outstripped by the growth of Birkenhead.

In those days fishermen lived in the villages of Ness, Little Neston, Leighton and Great Neston which included the hamlet of Parkgate, all of which came under Neston Parish. Their market was mainly local, supplying the many miners, farmers, brewers, blacksmiths, stonemasons etc., as well as lodging houses with fish, which in those days was plentiful and cheap.

Most of the boats were moored at Parkgate which was not a village in its own right, but a former port for Great Neston. The village was close to the gateway into the King's deer park, hence the name, Parkgate. It consisted of a number of houses and cottages, stretching from what is today the bottom of Station Road opposite the *Old Quay* pub, along the parade to the *Boathouse*. From Station Road to Mostyn Square was part of Great Neston and from Mostyn Square to the *Boathouse*, was part of Leighton. This long straggle of dwellings and inns stretching for over half a mile, was called Parkgate.

Pigot & Co's Directory published in 1830, records the following of Parkgate:
Parkgate is about a mile below Neston, and is of importance only as being the resort of visitors to it, in the bathing season. The houses which are neat and modern, are disposed in a long range, facing the estuary of the Dee. A regular ferry from hence to Flint affords great accommodation to those residing on the Welch [sic] shore, desirous of visiting Liverpool. A custom house is still supported, at Parkgate, but nearly the whole of its transactions are confined to vessels frequenting the contiguous collieries. About 15 years ago Parkgate partook of all the importance and bustle of a sea port, and at the time packets and other vessels were employed here in the trade with Ireland; but at this period, as a packet station, it is neglected, no vessel of berthen being enabled to approach within a considerable distance of the quay, from the large sand bank which occupies the channel. The population, which has increased since 1821, consisted then of about 400 persons.

The water in 1830 was too shallow for the Dublin packet to operate, but was deep enough for the smaller Flint and Bagillt ferry to reach Parkgate. The ferry tied up at the Leighton end of the quay, where the *Boathouse* is, and was met by coaches taking passengers to and from Liverpool and Chester.

Although as a port Parkgate was all but finished, there were still eight pubs and inns for the fishermen and travellers to choose from. They were the *Bulls Head, Flint & Bagillt Ferry House, Mostyn Arms Inn, Princess Royal, Red Lion, Sawyers Arms, Sir Thomas Picton* and the *White Lion*. The *Flint and Bagillt Ferry House* later became the *Boathouse & Pengwern Arms*.

The Neston men were inshore fishermen who went out and usually returned the same day with fish and shrimps for the local market. Their craft were two masted yawls, known locally as 'jigger boats', which were usually manned by two or three men.

By the 1850s Parkgate was finished as a port although the ferry service to and from Flint and Bagillt hung on until 1864. Some men who were previously mariners or boatmen took up fishing to earn a living rather than move to find work in other ports.

On the 1851 census, the following 23 men were recorded as being fishermen. Sometimes the houses or roads that people lived in are actually named in other cases it just gives the village or area. There might have been one or two more men out at sea when the census was taken on 31 March 1851.

NESS.			GREAT NESTON.		
NESS VILLAGE.			**NESTON VILLAGE**		
Lewis Robert	48	born L. Neston	Duncan Thomas	68	born Burton.
Thomas	25	Ness.	Henry	13	L. Neston
COLLIERY COTTAGES.			**CHESTER LANE.**		
Peers George	58	Puddington	Cross Willm.	40	L. Neston
			Jones Chris.	25	Ness Holt
LEIGHTON.			**PEMBERTONS GREEN.**		
			Mellor Willm.	74	Scotland.
PARKGATE.			Samuel	32	Neston.
Alderhead Rich.	19	born Parkgate	**LION YARD.**		
Bedson James	42	Leighton	Mellor James	42	Neston.
Bushell James	38	Liverpool	Parr Samuel	51	Ness.
Ludlow Thomas	26	Liverpool	**PARKGATE.**		
Matthews John	70	Neston	Peers George	35	Overpool.
Mealor Willm.	26	Ness	Bedson John	42	Neston.
Peers Samuel	23	Neston.	**ELDER COTTAGE.**		
			Matthews Rich.	40	Neston.
LITTLE NESTON.			Rich	17	Neston.
Campion Willm.	28	born L. Neston			

There were also two women from Ness and a lad from Little Neston recorded as being cockle gatherers. Many of the fishermen were inter-related. George Peers and Samuel Peers were the brothers of James Bushell's wife. This Peers family believed to have moved to Neston from Overpool near Ellesmere Port, during the 1820s. The address *Lion Yard* was where the *Golden Lion* pub was in Neston. As often happens due to people's accents and mishearing etc. some names are spelt wrongly; the name spelt Alderhead was almost certainly Ollerhead.

At this time fishermen were mainly engaged in catching fish rather than shrimps which were regarded as more of a luxury than a wholesome meal. Practically all the fish caught was eaten by local manual workers who liked a good sized fluke to get their teeth into. Some of the catch was hawked in nearby villages such as Thornton Hough and Willaston.

During the 1850s nearly half of the coal miners lived in Ness and a third lived in Little Neston. Taking into account the size of families in those days, it would appear that these villages would have been ideal for fishermen to operate from, yet only three fishermen lived in Ness and one in Little Neston, indicating that the silting up of the channel was by then serious enough to hinder the comings and goings of even small fishing boats. Fishermen had more or less abandoned Ness and Little Neston quays by about 1860 and were using Parkgate as an anchorage.

Just as in 1851, the 1861 census recorded 23 fishermen living in the area. None lived in Ness. At this time the Neston area was going through a rough patch. Ness and Little Neston mines had shut down and a few years later the Flint and Bagillt ferry service was stopped. There would have been a lot of poverty in the area and many locals were probably catching their own fish and raking for their own cockles and mussels.

In 1866 a railway line linking Parkgate and Neston to Birkenhead and Chester via Hooton was opened. Access to the railway network gave workers more chance of employment, and fishermen new and bigger markets. This caused a marked increase in the number of fishermen which nearly doubled, to a total of 43 by the year 1871 and are listed below; from the census taken on 3 April 1871.

```
LEIGHTON.                              GREAT NESTON.
---------                              --------------
PARKGATE                               BROOK STREET.
Bedson John       81  born Parkgate    Mellor Samuel     52        Neston.
       James     32        Parkgate    GOLDEN LION YARD.
Brierly Willm.   63        Neston      Fewtrell Geo.     26        Ellesmere
        Samuel   20        Neston      HIGH STREET.
Bushell James    59        Liverpool   Blundell James    17        Liverpool
Campion Willm.   54        Neston      Matthews John     18        Liverpool
        John     39        Neston      Mellor Samuel     22        Neston
Evans Rich.      38        Neston      Ollerhead Rich.   38        Neston
      Rich.      18        Parkgate              Robt.   28        Neston
      Samuel     40        Neston      Williams Thos.    25        Neston
Mealor James     20        Hallwood    BRIDGE STREET.
       John      52        Ness        Evans James       28        Neston
       Samuel    44        Ness        CHESTER ROAD.
Smith William    25        Neston      Mellor Jonath.    25        Neston
LEIGHTON COTTAGE.                      Peters Rich.      44        Neston
Sudlow Thos.     42        Liverpool   Peers Samuel      36        Neston
                                       Jones Chris.      46        L. Neston
LITTLE NESTON.                               Willm.      16        Parkgate
--------------                         PARKGATE.
Wood William     42        Neston      Bushell Robert    27        Parkgate
                                       Bedson John       63        Neston
THURSTASTON.                                  William    30        Parkgate
------------                                  Henry      19        Parkgate
DAWPOOL.                               Mahone William    22        Neston
Bedson James     61        Parkgate    Mathews Rich.     65        Neston
       James     23        Parkgate           Rich.      37        Neston
                                       Mealor William    49        Parkgate
                                              John       23        Leighton
                                              Thomas     16        Leigthton
                                       Mellor William    30        Neston
```

Parkgate fishermen James Bedson aged 61 and young James his 23 year old son, moved to the Dawpool area of Thurstaston for some reason where they are listed on the 1871 census of that village. Whatever reason took James to Dawpool did not keep him there as he is back on the Parkgate census list of 1881. Bedson is a very old Wirral name which is mentioned in documents relating to the Neston area in the 1600s.

By 1881 the number of fishermen had again risen, this time to 53. In Little Neston lived three fishermen, Neston 23, Parkgate 17 and in Leighton 10. The same local families continued to dominate the fishing industry. One or two other local families joined their ranks including James Ouldred, Thomas Price, William Milliner and Richard Murray. Out of the 53 fishermen only five were born outside the area. As well as James Bushell, Thomas Sudlow was also born in Liverpool. Thomas had been a fisherman in the area for over 30 years and learnt the trade from his uncle, old John Matthews from Neston. Another fisherman from outside the area was Thomas Robinson aged 29 from Manchester and the other two were 18 year olds, Job Littlemore of Tranmere and Robert Clarke of Birkenhead. These two teenagers lodged at Richard Peters' house in Cross Street. Although Job Littlemore was born in Tranmere, he came from a Neston family.

The number of fishermen living in Neston had increased from 14 to 23. They lived in Pykes Weint, Penningtons Yard, Bridge Street, Cross Street and nine lived in Chester Road. In those days Chester Road, formerly Chester Lane ran from High Street to the Chester High Road and included what later became Hinderton Road. Today Chester Road is only a few hundred yards long and runs from High Street, past the old picture house roughly as far as the bowling greens where it then becomes Hinderton Road.

During the 1880s things in the Parkgate / Neston area were looking up. The coal mines were busy again and in 1886 the railway network was extended from Parkgate through Heswall to West Kirby where it joined the Hoylake to Birkenhead and Wallasey line. Neston and Parkgate were now linked to Birkenhead, Liverpool and Chester on two lines. This gave greater scope to the fishermen. The demand for the delicacies of shrimps, cockles and mussels was beginning to rival the demand for fish. With a new mine opened and two railway systems linking the area to other towns and cities, the Neston area was on the up again. Some of the old hustle and bustle and former prosperity had returned. During the later 1880s there were upwards of about 66 fishermen, working from about 25 yawls.

Unfortunately the old enemy of Wirral's River Dee coast was closing in on Parkgate, having been been greatly speeded up by the digging of the New Cut. Silting, which had already put a stop to large vessels using the ports of Little Neston and Parkgate was now threatening the smaller fishing boats.

The silting and probable congestion at the three Parkgate slips persuaded some fishermen to move to the deeper waters of Heswall in the late 1880s. Not only did Heswall have a new railway link to Liverpool, but there was a growing local population to feed. Even fishermen from outside Wirral were attracted to Heswall.

In 1891 the number of fishermen recorded as living in the Neston area totalled 63 and in Heswall 10. About 30 fishing families lived in the Heswall and Neston areas, some with several branches and many were inter-related. Some men owned two or three boats.

Obviously many fishermen were married men, others were young sons, brothers and nephews working their families' boats and some lodged with boat owners families. Below is a list of fishermen with wives of those married and sons who were also fishermen, taken from the census of 6 April 1891.

```
LEIGHTON                                GREAT NESTON.
---------                               ------------
PARKGATE.                               NESTON VILLAGE.
Campion William    32    Neston         BIRCHES WEINT.
Brierly Samuel     40    Neston         Ollerhead Rich.   61    Neston
        Jane       41    Neston                   Mary    58    Neston
        John       18    Neston                   John    28    Neston
Evans Maurice      26    Neston                   Rich.   24    Neston
      Sarah        24    Neston                   Thos.   22    Neston
      Richard      22    Neston         CHESTER ROAD.
Higgins Willm.     45    Neston         Mellor Jonath.    44    Neston
        Marg.      35    Cardiff               Betsy      44    Neston
Jones Chris.       66    Neston                Jonath.    18    Neston
      Betsy        64    Neston         LION YARD.
Lewis John         52    Neston         Mellor Samuel     75    Neston
      Martha       47    Neston         LIVERPOOL ROAD.
      William      14    Neston         Murray Rich.      16    L. Neston
Matthews Thos.     34    Neston         CROSS STREET.
         Sarah     30    Neston         Peters Rich.      60    Neston
Mealor John        32    Neston                Jane       62    Neston
       Hannah      25    Heswall        BRIDGE STREET.
Mealor Samuel      59    Neston         Littlemore Job    42    Neston
       Ann         58    Neston                    Esther 39    Neston
Mealor William     41    Neston         PYKES WEINT.
       Mary        41    Neston         Evans James       50    Neston
Peers Samuel       66    Neston               Sarah       49.   Neston
      Mary         52    Stockport            James       18    Neston
Peters John        30    Neston               Samuel      15    Neston
       Ellen       29    Neston         Fewtrell Geo.     46    Colpoint
Peters William     36    Neston                  Betsy    48    Neston
```

	Ann	34	Neston	Geo.	23	Neston
Robinson Thos.		36	Neston	Willm.	19	Neston
	Anne	34	Neston	Mellor Samuel	43	Neston
Roscoe Daniel		30	Neston	Anne	43	Neston
	Mary	28	Neston	George	16	Neston
Smith Joseph		18	Neston	PARKGATE.		
Whitehead Wm.		18	Chester	Bedson George	35	Neston
				Brierly Willm.	58	Neston
LITTLE NESTON.				Kate	58	Neston
----------------				Bushell Robert	48	Neston
Ollerhead Robt.		18	Neston	Sarah	46	Chester
Peers Thomas		26	Neston	Campion John	58	Neston
	John	18	Neston	Mary	59	Neston
Peters Rich.		29	L. Neston	John	36	Liverpool
Roscoe Willm.		39	L. Neston	James	13	Neston
	Mary A.	37	Neston	Edge William	17	Caldy
	Thomas	17	L. Neston	Higgins Benj.	36	Neston
Wellings Harry		39	Montgomery	Jane	34	Whitehav.
	Jane	34	L. Neston.	Lewis James	28	Neston
				Mary	27	Neston
				Rich.	16	Rainford
				Maddox James	21	Halewood
				Milner Willm.	33	Neston
				Charlot	31	Neston
				Webster Henry	23	Neston
				Smith William	45	Neston
				Sarah	45	Neston
				John	22	Neston
				James	18	Neston
				Richard	15	Neston

The above list illustrates just how localised the fishing industry was. Even the odd 'foreigner' was married to a Neston girl such as Harry Wellings from Montgomery. Harry lived in Little Neston where he originally came as a coal miner and must have opted for a healthier occupation. William Milner listed above is the same man recorded as William Milliner 10 years earlier. There were also two retired fishermen recorded, John Mealor aged 73, grandfather of 18 year old Joseph Smith listed above who lived with him, and 79 year old James Bushell living with his son Robert. The above Samuel Brierly had another son, 16 year old George who was a fish hawker. Many a young son hawked fish round the houses to bring in ready cash, before becoming full-time fishermen when they were older.

HESWALL FISHERMEN AND WIVES 1891.

STATION COTTAGES.			CABIN ON THE SHORE.		
Bedson John	50	Neston	Bedson James	58	Parkgate
Brierly Willm.	31	Neston	Eliza	43	Liverpool
Susan	32	Neston	HESWALL SLACK.		
Evans Samuel	28	Neston	Bucklay John	42	Chester
Margaret	25	Chirk	Eliza	41	Chester
Rigby James	48	Southport	John	15	Chester
Margaret	52	Southport			
John	27	Southport			
Taylor Joseph	26	Neston			
Mary	28	Chester			
Williams John	35	Neston			
Sarah	47	Neston			

There might have been one or two fishermen missed out as they could have been at sea or away somewhere when the census was taken. One such fisherman was 25 year old Thomas Evans of Parkgate who was recorded on the 1891 census of Thurstaston. Thomas was staying at the home of his girl friend Alice Roberts who lived at *Hillside Farm*, which is still standing in

School Lane, near the *Heatherland* restaurant. Thomas married Alice in 1892 and they lived at *Marlfield Cottage* which Alice owned. In 1915 Thomas was killed whilst serving as Chief Quartermaster and Helmsman on the *Lusitania* which was torpedoed by a German U-boat off the Irish coast on 7 May 1915. His descendants live in *Marlfield Cottage*, Pensby Road to this day.

As can be noted from the lists of names and addresses of fishermen, the person or persons who took the details of Heswall and Neston was more conscientious and noted actual addresses. Whoever took the details of Little Neston, Parkgate and Leighton did not bother to note the street or house names and everyone who was born locally was recorded as being born in Neston, although many were born in Little Neston and Leighton etc.

Station Cottages, where many of the Heswall fishermen lived were pulled down years ago. This old terrace of 12 cottages was known locally as the *Flukebone* and stood close to the old Heswall Railway Station, now part of the Wirral Way.

Some fishermen decided that they would be better off leaving the Wirral side of the Dee and settling in ports with deeper waters on the Welsh side. During the 1880s and 1890s members of the Evans and Mealor families stowed their belongings on their boats and sailed away from Parkgate and Heswall and settled in Flint and Bagillt. Lemuel Evans moved to Bagillt and eventually in 1895 his elderly father Samuel joined him. Samuel took bad and died a few days before Christmas. Lemuel towed his father's body back to Heswall in a little punt behind his yawl, for burial at the church of St. Peter, patron saint of fishermen. Today there are still descendants of these Heswall and Parkgate families fishing from the Welsh side of the Dee.

The boom in fishing, shown by the 1871 and 1891 census figures at Heswall and Parkgate, kept a number of men employed building boats in their own small yards. Two such men were Richard Tickle of Hadlow Road, Willaston and Joseph Cottrell of High Street, Neston.

As time went on the new Heswall fishing community grew as families left the Neston / Parkgate areas and moved to *Station Cottages* and Park West. One of the Brierly family was said to have gone to live in Newfoundland where he became a very successful salmon fisherman and made his fortune. On returning to Wirral in the 1890s, he was reputed to have bought a large quantity of bricks and tiles from Buckley Brickworks. Brierly shipped them over to Heswall on a barge which he beached at Banks Road.

On a long narrow strip of land which was once an enclosure belonging to the Lords of the Manor of Heswall, Brierly began building. This enclosure, measuring two roods and 29 perches, ran almost the length of Banks Road. By 1899 he had built the houses numbered one to five at the top end of the road and during the early 1900s he built the six lower down. Some of these houses became the homes of fishermen.

At the turn of the century both the Parkgate and Heswall boats continued to bring in good catches. During the early decades of this century most of the fishermen changed over from fishing in two-masted yawls or 'jigger boats' to 'nobbies', properly called Morecambe Bay Prawners. Nobbies had both sail and engine and were obviously easier to handle as with engines they did not have to rely on favourable winds.

In 1914 no fishing boat owners or part-owners were recorded in directories as living in Neston, Ness or Little Neston, only Parkgate and Heswall. In Parkgate lived 16 fishing boat owners or part owners from 10 families. In Heswall only two families are recorded, Evans and Lewis, who had a number of boats and quite a few family members working them.

Slowly but surely the number of fishing families was dwindling. Although the number of Parkgate fishermen boatowners recorded in Kelly's 1923 Directory was up to 18, only nine families were now involved. It appears that the missing family were the Matthews who had fished the Dee for generations. In Heswall the Evans and Lewis families were still recorded.

In 1927 a field near Heswall shore, called *Lydiate Gutter*, owned about 150 years ago by Charlotte Ann Davenport who rented it to William Totty, was sold for building. A road of houses called Mostyn Avenue was built by local builders Jones and Hough. Among the first occupants was the family of Ciggy Wakelam who tells me that his father bought their house for £320.

Many of these houses along with some in Banks Road which ran parallel, became the homes of fishermen. Some moved in from nearby *Station Cottages* and others from Parkgate, forming a fishing community known locally as *The Bonks*.

During the 1920s Parkgate fishermen concentrated on shrimps, cockles, mussels and fluke. A large amount of these were sold in tea rooms and along the Parade to the many day trippers who came by rail and bus. Tons of shellfish were also sent by rail to the cities. Heswall fishermen sent most of their catch by rail, direct to Liverpool market but some was sold to fishmongers Rob Tarbuck of Pensby Road and Evelyn Sissons of The Mount.

Cockles and mussels were gathered along the local beaches in large quantities. There was a mussel bed opposite the Dungeon and another large one on Heswall shore, opposite Park West. Often whole families, including women and children went 'scrattin' shellfish together. They walked to these beds along the sands with their donkeys to pick and transport home what they could sell. Sometimes they walked to the cockle beds at Leasowe and loaded cockles onto flat-backed carts.

In 1928 a newspaper article reported that boat loads of mussels were flooding the markets of Liverpool, Birkenhead and the big Lancashire towns at the expense of the fishermen based in the Parkgate area. This was basically put down to the fact that, although the demand for shellfish was expanding in leaps and bounds, the Dee fishemen were not cashing in on it as they should have been doing. The article blamed the reluctance of our local fishermen to use modern advertising and marketing methods as well as their preference for operating in independant groups rather than combining to work more efficiently.

Of Parkgate / Heswall shellfish the following statements were made in the Birkenhead News in 1928;
Shrimps, probably of the the best quality obtainable anywhere round our coast, are to be had in unlimited quantities off Parkgate. The demand also is unlimited, but there is no properly organised connecting link whereby fresh shrimps in abundance can be brought to the doorstep of the consumer... Parkgate posseses the best grade of shrimps and mussels. Ton loads are dispatched annually by rail to Yorkshire towns, but the volume of trade is infinitesimal compared with what it would be if the distribution were put on an up to date basis and customers were supplied direct from the port... Unfortunately, some Parkgate fishermen have been loath to take advantage of facilities for ensuring the sterilisation of their mussel catches, one instance of the unwillingness to break away from the old conventions and adopt those modern methods which pave the way to successful trade... "Parkgate shrimps and Parkgate mussels for Merseyside" should be the slogan for Parkgate fishermen.

However it appears that the local authority was holding back the Parkgate shellfish industry. In October 1928 an appeal was made in Neston Town Hall by Mr. Algernon George Grenfell M.A. of Mostyn House, on behalf of the local fishermen who had been refused permission by the U.D.C. to build a shed at the Boathouse end of the Promenade, near the slipway, for boiling and bottling shellfish. Mr. H.G. Williams for Neston Council said that *"the shed would set a precedent that the area was industrial"*.

It seems that the Council would not admit that fishing was an industry. On one hand authorities wanted stricter health controls on seafood, and on the other hand local authorities wanted to deny their own fishermen and ratepayers the modern facilities to provide properly sterilised sea food.

Parkgate shrimps were potted and sold in tubs which were sent all over the country by small family concerns who worked from the home. Before potting, the shrimps were tipped into pans of warm butter, then put out onto a plate. Once cool, the butter coated shrimps were put in tubs which were sealed with butter and a piece of greaseproof paper. Some families added their own little extra flavouring, such as the Bushell family who sprinkled the pans of shrimps with mace.

Sometimes fishermen made some unusual catches, such as the one made by Mr. Fewtrell of Parkgate. On 6 June 1928 Mr. Fewtrell hauled in his nets whilst fishing in the River Dee, and found he had caught an octopus. William Fewtrell, the fisherman's nephew took it home to Richmond Terrace. The oldest fisherman in the village was asked about the catch and said he could not remember an octopus ever being caught. It was described as being grey and with a hard back like a shell and two large tentacles about 18 inches long with large suckers on the ends. It also had several small tentacles with suckers and the body was like a bag. The creature was taken by bus to Prenton for examination and put into a tank. Unfortunately it died the next day.

During the 1920s and 30s, although the fishermen sailing from Parkgate and Heswall were still operating in small family concerns, they were making a reasonable living. They were more fortunate than the local miners who had seen Wirral Colliery close, never to be re-opened.

Fishermen unloading their catch at the Middle Slip, Parkgate.

The silting of the channel at Parkgate was now extremely serious and the water was getting shallower and shallower, but still the remaining fishing families kept operating from their home port as their forefathers had done. It was the life and a livelihood they had been bred into.

Another old fishing family was missing from the list by 1934, the name of Lemuel Mellor was not listed. The founder of this fishing family was Scottish mariner, William Mellor who in 1799 married Mary Norman of Neston. He probably met Mary whilst his ship was visiting

Parkgate or Neston from his home port of Ayr. William settled in Neston and eventually became a fisherman, probably after the port's decline. However another name had joined the ranks of the Parkgate fishermen, John Cross. A fisherman called William Cross had lived in Neston in 1851, and John Cross could have been a descendant.

Although only nine families were fishing from Parkgate in 1934 the same number as in 1923, their numbers had risen to 20, the Mealors for instance had five fishermen in the family and the Peters four. There was not much employment in the area at this time so probably fishing the family boats was the only option.

In Heswall five members of the Evans family and two members of the Lewis family were fishing. The water in Gayton Gutter was still deep and the Heswall men were not experiencing the navigational problems of their friends and relations two and a half miles up river at Parkgate.

During the 1930s came the crunch for the fishermen of Parkgate. The silting of the river was beginning to make it impossible for them to come and go as they wanted and needed to. It was obvious that the days of a local fishing fleet using Parkgate as the home port were over.

By the late 1930s it was clear that the fishermen would soon have to give up, or operate from deeper waters lower down the river. Many of the young members of fishing families were looking to other industries for employment.

In 1939 there were only 12 Parkgate boat owners or part boat owners, from eight families, a fall of eight men and one family equalling 40% in only five years. Thomas Robinson of Parkgate Parade, whose family had moved from Manchester to Neston over 60 years before was not recorded in the 1939 list.

The Parkgate fishermen and boat owners recorded in the 1939 Directory are listed below.

Bushell Thomas, Dover Cottage.	Mealor John, Hill View.
Campion William, Station Road.	Peters Henry, Station Road.
Cross Henry, Parkgate.	Peters James, Mostyn Terrace.
Fewtrell William, Station Road.	Peters Richard, The Parade.
Higgins Fred, The Parade.	Smith James, Station Road.
Mealor George, New Cottage.	Smith Joseph, The Parade.

These remaining fishermen usually crewed their boats with relations from the local area. As always much of the shellfish was sold along Parkgate Parade and in the fishmongers of Samuel Mealor and Joseph Smith in Neston High Street; the rest went by train to Chester and cities in Lancashire and Yorkshire.

In Heswall the Evans and Lewis families were still fishing from Banks Road and Mostyn Avenue. Richard Evans was also building and repairing boats at his yard at the bottom of Banks Road. The Heswall fishermen still went out for fish rather than shrimps. Their catch was, as always, sent to Liverpool Market but some was sold locally, as usual by Rob Tarbuck in the Top Village and by Drew's fishmongers in the Bottom Village. Also Neston hawkers bought quantities of fish from Heswall and took them by train to sell on housing estates, outside factories and some even went to villages in Wales. Some Neston women loaded fish on donkeys and walked as far as Rock Ferry, Eastham and Ellesmere Port to hawk them.

During the Second World War the Parkgate fishermen were asked to concentrate on catching fish and not the delicacies of shrimps and shell-fish. With food rationing, fish catches were an important wholesome family food. Fishermen of an age for military service served in the Royal Navy in both World Wars. All the young men of the Evans family served a full six years in the Navy, leaving only the older men and boys to carry on fishing.

By the 1940s fishermen could no longer moor their boats at Parkgate and had to find anchorages in the deeper waters of Heswall, Thurstaston, Caldy or Hoylake. During the 1950s the marsh spread over Parkgate sands. Pollution had also become a problem owing to the great rise in the populations of Heswall and Neston as well as what was washed in from Liverpool Bay.

It takes a special kind of man to live the hard life of a fisherman, particularly in winter and when, after all that hard effort, a regular wage is not earned it must be very disheartening. As the old fishermen died or retired their trade was seldom carried on by younger members of their families. Most fishing families gave up their ancestors way of life and found alternative work. This was not easy for them, but the lure of regular money in other, more reliable industries, understandably drew them away, although some still fished part-time.

The Higgins family wanted to carry on fishing and moved to Heswall where the fishermen were having a better time of it. Bill 'Wracko' Higgins was quite a character, he earned his nickname by finding or somehow arriving first on the scene at any wreck in the River Dee estuary area. In the local dialect, wreck was pronounced wrack.

The Nancy sailing the Dee.
Originally the Lewis family boat, in the above picture, owned and sailed by Mr. D. Brierley.

During the late 1950s and early 1960s the Heswall fishermen changed from catching fish to concentrate on shrimping. The quality and quantity of fish caught in the Dee and Liverpool bay was not what it was. Over-fishing and pollution were blamed. During the 1950s there were three families fishing from Heswall;

```
MOSTYN AVENUE.                          THE MOORINGS.
Evans  Ben                              Evans Maurice
       Bill     number 31                     'Shiner'   Dee Cott
       Bill     number 19               BANKS ROAD
       Henry    number 21               Lewis Charlie
       Laddie   number 28               Evans Dick       number 2.
BROAD LANE.                             MANNERS LANE.
Evans  Jack     number 4                Higgins 'Wracko'
```

At this time much of their catch went to farmer's wife, Jinny Sissons who was an Evans before marriage. Jinny lived in the old white cottage on the opposite corner to the *Shrewsbury Arms* on the Chester High Road, the yard of which was used as a fish and shrimp clearing house. She lived and breathed fishing and organised the buying and selling and distribution of vast quantities of shrimps.

In the very hard winter of 1963 three nobbies were sunk by ice-flows whilst moored at Caldy. One of these was the *Annie* belonging to Albert Peters of 14 Mostyn Gardens, Parkgate. Half the Heswall fishing fleet was crushed by ice. The remaining nobbies were beached at Banks Road, Heswall where all the fishermen got together and hauled them ashore with ropes.

Fishermen on Heswall Shore during the Big Freeze of 1963.
Left to right; the Evans brothers Laddie, Jack and Henry, far left looking across the river is Dick.

During the later 1960s the shrimping industry began to decline, owing to serious pollution. As the remaining fishermen retired, they either sold their boats or else worked them part-time with their lads, more as a way of life that they didn't want to let go.

In the late 1960s and early 1970s, fish and shrimps were still regularly sold in Heswall pubs. A good sized bag of shrimps cost half-a-crown (12½p) in 1967, fish and chips were one shilling and sixpence (7½p), and a pint of bitter in the bar was one shilling and 10 pence (9p). On darts nights in the *Dee View*, fisherman Dick Evans, manager of our darts team used to fetch fresh shrimp butties for the lads. In the *Sandon Arms* shrimps were sold by Lal Higgins who worked at John Summers Steel Works but still kept his family tradition going and fished part-time.

In those days most of the remaining Heswall fishermen drank in the *Black Horse* as they had always done. The *Dee View* was regarded as a 'lads' pub, which it largely was, although young at heart Dick Evans and a few other men of his age enjoyed a bit of banter there with the young'ns. If we left the *Black Horse* (which is a Bents house) to have a pint in the *Dee View* (which was Birkenhead Brewery), the fishermen used to take the mickey out of us. They would say things like "Oh aye, too strong is it, going for a drop o'lads ale 'ey?"

The older men often spoke with strong local accents and used to say some funny things. Old Jim Lewis sometimes substituted an A for an O as many did who spoke the local dialect, such as in bonk for bank and mon for man. I stood next to him once when he asked a young student working behind the bar for a pint of bitter and an 'omlet. The lad came back and said "I've searched the crisp boxes and there is no such flavour as omelette". Jim shook his head in disgust and said, "it's not crisps I want lad, it's an 'omlet cigar".

Today there is only one full time fisherman living in Parkgate. But many of the old fishing families such as the Bushells still live locally. The Bushell family had fished the Dee since the 1830s when James Bushell moved from Liverpool to Parkgate where he worked his boat. James' grandson Thomas, had three boats at one stage, including the well known *Hearts of Oak*. His wife Clara, nee Shaw, gave him four sons and four daughters. Three of his sons became plasterers due to the decline in fishing. They were well-known characters and keen wildfowlers who practically lived on the marsh when hard winters put a stop to building work. Thomas, of *Dover Cottage,* Station Road, died during the 1940s. His son Reg, who once lived in the *Watch House* was the last fisherman in the family. Today members of the Bushell family still live in Parkgate and probably will for some time to come. The sea is still in their blood. Fred, James Bushell's great, great-grandson, is an engineer who sailed in the Merchant Navy and lives in Bowring Drive, with his wife and children.

Descendants of Parkgate fishermen are going strong all over Wirral. One such descendant whose roots go back over 200 years, is hair-dresser Garry Mellor. Garry, who lives in Thingwall Drive, Irby with his wife and children, is a direct descendant of Scottish fisherman William Mellor and grandson of Jonathan Mellor of Parkgate and Maud Saxon of Heswall.

The last Parkgate fisherman is Colin Mealor whose family originally came from Ness. Colin sails from Thurstaston and sells shrimps from his shop on Parkgate Parade.

The last Heswall fisherman is Henry Evans who I have known since we were lads. Henry's family have been fishermen for generations. His father, old Henry, was a fisherman all his life, and his mother Cissy, nee Smith, is a Neston miner's daughter. Henry tells me that during the 1700s his family moved from North Wales, to Parkgate where they were mariners. They also ran a beerhouse called the *Turf Tavern*, lodging houses, and the *Sawyers Arms* pub for about 50 years. During most of that period the *Sawyers Arms* was run by mariner Maurice Evans who was born in Parkgate in 1800. There are several branches of the Evans family and some time between the 1880s and the early 1900s they moved from Parkgate to Heswall and moored their boats in the deeper waters of Gayton Gutter.

Today Henry Evans only moors his nobby in the 'safe haven' of Heswall's Gayton Gutter during mid winter. The silting of the estuary now prevents anyone working from Heswall regularly, as it is only possible to sail in and out of Gayton Gutter at high tide, every 12 hours. This is very inconvenient and time consuming. By mooring his nobby two and a half miles away in the deeper waters of Thurstaston, Henry can sail out on the flood tide and return on the ebb of the same tide. These short shrimping trips usually take about six or seven hours.

Henry quite often trawls for shrimps in the traditional fishing grounds of East Hoyle Bank off Hilbre, as his father and uncles did a generation before. His nobby has a 22 horse-power Lister engine which only uses three or four gallons of diesel a day. Once underway, Henry carefully lets his trawl net out overboard, taking care not to let it turn upside down. The net is just like a big mesh sack and is towed or rather trawled behind the nobby. Fish and shrimps enter the net through the open end and are caught in the bottom.

Nobby boats are very low in the water. The short drop makes the handling of nets and the haul back aboard easier. These days Henry uses nylon nets and ropes which last far longer than those made with the traditional materials, but they are cold and very hard on the hands. Net rope rollers are now made of nylon and not wood, but one thing that has never changed on Henry's boat is the 'iron man', better known as the capstan. A capstan is an essential piece of equipment, enabling a fisherman to winch a full net aboard. The capstan aboard Henry's nobby was bought in Southport by his grandfather over 70 years ago.

After landing the net containing his catch on deck, Henry separates the crabs and fish from the shrimps and then riddles them. The riddle he uses is the old 'thru'penny ha'penny riddle', so called because the width of the gap in the wire mesh was measured with three old pennies and a half-penny on edge. After riddling, the decks are then swilled down with buckets of sea water to wash the seaweed and small fish overboard through holes in the side called scuppers. Any big crabs are left to crawl overboard through the scuppers.

Whilst homeward bound Henry boils the shrimps in sea water on his calor gas boiler mounted on deck. The shrimps are done when they turn pink with a few white speckles on their backs. Years ago this operation was very hazardous in rough weather as the boilers were coal fired and mounted on the cabin top, and many a fisherman was scalded in years gone by.

After arriving back at Thurstaston, Henry ties his nobby to the moorings and comes ashore by dinghy with his catch of shrimps. On the beach he puts the dinghy on his trailer and tows it back home to Heswall and down Scabbrook Hill to The Bonks.

Henry's nobby is his pride and joy. He keeps it ship-shape and seaworthy. Sailing and fishing are in his blood, they are his hobbies and the life he was born to. Taking his lads out fishing and showing them the ropes gives Henry great pleasure. For the past five years an annual nobby race has been held at Conwy in which only sail is used. Last year Henry and his sons young Henry and Sam took on all opposition and won. There have been a number of nobby races from Liverpool in which Henry has participated.

As a lad Henry fished off Iceland in the big trawlers and his lad, young Henry, has followed in his footsteps. Young Henry has worked on the bigger trawlers from Conwy and the East Coast. Just before Christmas 1995 he was in hospital after nearly being drowned when the trawler he was working on capsized in a gale. That near tragedy is one of the many hazards fishermen face all their working lives.

The Evans family, like all other old fishing families, have been involved in their share of tragedies. In July 1907 Richard (Dick) Evans aged 21 of *Station Cottages,* Heswall, was lost in the River Dee off Dawpool. Dick fell overboard and drowned whilst helping his father to haul in the nets. His father searched in vain for young Dick and eventually had to return home to his family with the terrible tidings. His body was washed up at Dawpool about a week later.

In December 1932, during a gale, Henry's father and uncle Dick cut fellow fisherman Bob Price loose from the mast of his wrecked nobby, north of West Hoyle Bank. Unfortunately Bob had died of exposure and the body of his shipmate Bill Lewis was never found.

All through the ages people have been lost off our local coast; these sad happenings are to be seen in the records of several Wirral churches. Below are listed a few burials at the church of St. Mary and St. Helen in Neston during Parkgate's heyday as a port;

1804 Eric Jonsen, a Dane from Christiana, lost on the sands of Parkgate.

1806 A total of 27 crew and passengers, including the Master, Thomas Walker, lost in the *King George* packet, buried after being washed ashore over a period of several months. (The *King George* packet was lost on 14 September 1806 near Hoyle Bank, with over 100 persons aboard, of which only three or four people survived).

1808 John Davies died of fatigue from shipwreck.

1810 William Price, Joseph Richardson, Mary Coterall and Catherine Jones alias Roberts, lost in a boat.

1810 William Peters drowned attempting to cross the Dee.

The year 1810 was a particularly bad year for Wirral fishermen. On Christmas Day and Boxing Day of that year seven Hoose fishermen were buried at West Kirby Church; four were members of the Bird family and three from the Hughes family.

Although hazardous, to the Mealors and the Evans', fishing the waters of the River Dee is a family tradition, which I hope they can keep up for generations to come.

The Gee Whiz belonging to Colin Mealor of Parkgate and the Blue Circle belonging to Henry Evans junior of Heswall in Gayton Gutter at high tide, June 1996.

NESTON COAL MINES

The only coal mines in Wirral were in the Neston area, situated close to the River Dee in Ness and Little Neston. The first pits were opened in the Denhall area of Ness. In the later 1700s mining was also carried out in Little Neston from pits at the bottom of what was then Wood Lane, later known as Colliery Lane and now called Marshlands Road.

Coal was dug in Ness / Little Neston thousands of years ago. At the Romano - British excavation in Irby, small pieces of coal have been found in the remains of a primitive smithying hearth along with pieces of iron waste. I spoke to Rob Philpott, the archaeologist in charge of the dig, who said that the coal was probably from the Neston area, but could have been bartered from a settlement on the Welsh side of the Dee. To prove exactly where it came from I went to Little Neston and took sample pieces of coal from various parts of the slag heaps. Rob sent the samples to British Coal laboratories to be analysed. The answer came back that the coal from the Romano - British site was identical to that from the slag heaps, thus proving that man had been using coal from the Ness / Little Neston area for at least 2,000 years.

Coal was probably first found on the surface and open-cast mined by early man. Open-cast or open-pit mining was carried out by simply digging holes or trenches down into outcrops of coal lying near the surface.

Ness and Neston were originally Viking settlements which probably took their names from the nearby *Ness* or headland of Burton Point which jutted out into the River Dee. The hamlet of Denhall was originally called *Danewell*, an ancient watering place. Viking smiths in Wirral would have used Denhall coal in their furnaces when making tools and weapons.

Ness is mentioned in the Domesday Book written in 1086, but there is no reference to any coal pits, only farmland, the whole township being valued at 16 shillings (80p). Over the centuries villagers in the Ness area probabaly dug coal in small quantities by open-cast mining for domestic use. People from further afield would have only gone to the trouble of obtaining coal for specific reasons, such as metal-working.

It was not until the 1600s and 1700s that coal was dug for sale on a larger scale. J.H. Hodson wrote that two small pits were worked in the early 1600s. These pits would have been open-cast but deeper down as all the coal on the surface would have been mined by this time. Coal found deeper down, but still at reasonably shallow depths, say between 50 and 300 feet, was often reached by sloping tunnels known as drifts. Another method of mining shallow depth coal in the 1600s was from 'bell pits'. In the North West they were called 'bottle pits'. These were holes dug down until coal was reached and then widened out into the coal seam, making bottle shaped holes. The coal was hauled up either by a pony or by men using winding gear. This primitive method of mining coal was used as late as the 1920s by striking miners to obtain coal for themselves from land not owned by the bosses.

It is said that during the 1600s, Ness coal was carried to the surface in hundredweight (112 pound) baskets, up rock steps cut up sloping tunnels from depths of over 100 feet. The only light was from the mouth of the tunnel with a few candles here and there during a working day of up to 12 hours.

Wirral historians say that coal was first commercially mined from deep tunnel mines in the Denhall area of Ness when the Stanley's of Hooton opened a colliery between 1750 and 1760. There was no local labour who knew anything about underground coal mining, so to begin with the Stanley family brought in skilled miners, mainly from North Wales and Lancashire. Sulley states that the pit was opened in 1760, Mortimer says 1757, other authorities say 1750. However, it appears that the mine opened earlier than this as the church records of St. Mary and St. Helen in Neston record the following baptisms; *1746 James, son of George Gregory, miner, of the parish of Holywell in Wales and his wife Jane; 1749 Mary, daughter of John Neilly, a miner of Great Neston, and Alice his wife.*

During the 1750s Denhall Colliery employed a fair number of men but being a port and a country town, there were more men in the Neston area employed as mariners and in agriculture. There were also smaller numbers of men working at every trade, including slaters, shoemakers, brewers, millers, sadlers, weavers, coopers, blacksmiths etc., a few fishermen and, surprisingly, quite a few soldiers. At this time a large number of Irish workers lodged in the area.

In these early days colliers worked at several tasks. 'Hewers' hacked the coal from the coal face, for the 'drawer' who shovelled the coal into tubs which the 'getter' pulled from the working face to the shaft bottom, where a 'banksman gave instructions and guided the load of coal which was winched up by the 'winder'.

Raising coal from a bottle mine.

One of the first pits to be worked was called *Bank Heys* and some of the coal was supplied to big houses of the well-to-do, all over Wirral. In 1768, my direct ancestor John Dawson, Yoeman of Irby and Moreton, made a land rental agreement with Sir Philip Egerton of *Leasowe Castle* and Oulton. The agreement was a yearly rent of £82 for an estate in Moreton called *Cookes Tenement* and one of the many conditions in the document concerned Ness coal. The following condition was stipulated:

And further that he, the said John Dawson, shall and will, at his own expense yearly and every year during the continuance of this demise, draw from Ness Colliery or such coal pits as shall be appointed by the said Philip Egerton his heirs or assigns, not exceeding twenty five statute miles distant, set and lay down on such a day as shall be appointed by the said Philip Egerton, his heirs or assigns, on three days notice being given or left for that purpose at the messuage hereby demised, one good waggon load of coals. He the said Philip Egerton or his heirs paying for such coals at the pits or paying the said John Dawson for them on delivery. And also shall and will on the like notice, deliver yearly at Oulton aforesaid, one other waggon load. The said Philip Egerton his heirs or assigns paying for such coals at the pits or on delivery and also paying for the carrying thereof after the rate of shillings per ton if brought from the coal pits.

During the 1760s *Denhall Quay* was built for the purpose of loading ships with coal for export. Some coal was shipped to towns in North and South Wales which were more easily accessible by sea than over hills and mountains using the rough tracks and roads. Most Ness coal was shipped to Ireland and the Isle of Man where no coal is to be found, only peat.

Baronet Sir Thomas Stanley of *Denna Hall* not only worked his own pits in the Denhall area of Ness but leased some from Thomas Cottingham of Little Neston. After a number of years of mining, shafts extended for over a mile under the River Dee.

In about 1791 Stanley had two underground canals cut to enable him to transport coal in boats from various parts of his mines to the pit shafts for winding up to the surface. Mortimer states that one canal was 60 yards below the surface and the other 94. Stanley probably learned of this method of transporting coal from his Lancashire miners from Wigan and Worsley who had used underground canals for years.

The colliers hacked lumps of coal away from under the coal face with picks to undermine it. Then, by hammering and turning long straight metal spikes with sharpened tips, they hammer-drilled holes in the coal face. These drill holes were packed with gunpowder and the coal was blasted from the face. The huge lumps of coal were then broken up with picks and shovelled into baskets aboard the long narrow flat-bottomed boats. Men propelled the boats along at about one mile an hour by lying on the baskets of coal and pushing against the roof of the tunnel with their feet.

Miners 'walking' a loaded coal punt along the underground canal at Ness mine.

Miners in those days were paid on a piece work basis at so much per hundredweight. Lancashire miners from the Wigan area might have established the free coal system in Ness, which they enjoyed in their home town. The free coal system eventually spread nationwide and was originally measured as 12 hundredweight for the boss and one for the miner. These men could neither read nor write and to record how much coal they produced they put their own special tags or markers in the baskets which were counted on the surface.

Neston had for a long time been the most populous area in Wirral owing to its shipping and mines. Neston Parish consisted of eight villages, Great Neston, Little Neston, Ness, Leighton, Willaston, Raby, Thornton Mayou (later Hough) and Ledsham. In those days half of what is now Parkgate was within the boundaries of Great Neston and the other half was part of Leighton. The chart below records the population figures for Neston Parish in 1811.

VILLAGE	HOUSES	AGRIC.	TRADE	OTHER	MALE	FEMALE	TOTAL	FAMILIES
Great Neston	325	20	200	109	609	723	1,332	329
Leighton	57	30	15	12	104	183	287	57
Little Neston	56	56	0	0	117	126	243	56
Ness	52	49	2	1	293	169	462	52
Willaston	39	41	0	0	89	92	181	41
Thornton Mayou	36	25	4	7	87	92	179	36
Raby	24	22	0	2	83	67	150	24
Ledsham	14	13	1	0	41	34	75	14

Just how big and important the Neston area was is shown by its comparison with other villages at the time such as Wallasey with a population of 440, West Kirby 141 and Birkenhead with only 105 inhabitants.

The chart records the number of home owners or tenants engaged in three areas of employment, firstly, agriculture, secondly trades including manufacturing and handicraft and thirdly others. The category of 'others' would be mainly mariners, fishermen, soldiers and miners.

In most country villages, the numbers of males and females was pretty well even except for slight differences where gangs of Irishmen were hired for seasonal farmwork or a number of big houses employed several servant girls. This is true of the villages recorded on the chart except for Great Neston, Leighton and Ness. These figures indicate two things regarding those three villages. The larger number of females compared to males in Great Neston and Leighton was probably due to so many mariners, particularly from the Parkgate area, being away at sea when the census was taken. On the other hand, the large number of males compared to females in Ness was almost certainly due to miners lodging there.

The chart shows that the population of Ness was extremely high for its number of houses. By comparison, in Little Neston there were four more houses but only half the population. This probably points to the fact that in the mining village of Ness, a large number of miners from outside the area were lodging with farming families. Farm labourers and small holders in Ness would have been very poor, and so some of their sons would have worked in the mines and rent from lodgers was a great help to the family income. Overcrowding and public health must have been serious problems.

At this time it appears there were two small mines operated by two local men. Land tax documents of Little Neston for several years up to 1812 record Thomas Sharpe and Thomas Cottrell both registered as colliers and paying land tax on property. The Cottrell family were registered as colliers for about 20 years.

In 1812 Baronet Sir Thomas Stanley put his mines up for sale and the following advertisement was placed in the Courant;
To be let for any term not exceeding 30 years, Ness Colliery close to the River Dee where coals are shipped off an extensive and convenient Quay for Ireland, North and South Wales and

the Isle of Man. Together with a farm of about 90 statute acres etc. adjoining the works etc. The coal consists of three veins of 6, 5 and 7 feet respectively, as well as one of 2 feet. Under the last is a seam of excellent fire brick clay etc. etc. For further particulars application should be made to Mr. Ashurst of Puddington.
No buyer came forward.

It was stated in the 1822 Ness Colliery lawsuit that, in 1819, Stanley's lease on Thomas Cottingham's Little Neston mine ran out and Mr. Cottingham decided to work his mines himself. The coal mines belonging to Stanley and Cottingham were working some of the same seams. The two mines were to stop working at the boundary of Ness and Little Neston so as not to encroach on one another's property. Mr. Cottingham was suspicious that part of the canal which Stanley had dug, was over his boundary and in Little Neston. In November 1819 Mr. Cottingham employed an underground surveyor to asses the situation. With the aid of a miner's compass the surveyor proved that part of Stanleys tunnel was in fact cut into Little Neston and therefore trespassed on Mr. Cottinghams ground. Mr. Cottingham took Baronet Stanley to court for trespass and was awarded £100 damages. This court case led to much bad feeling.

In 1821 Stanley sent men down his own number 6 pit in Ness which led into an underground road in Cottingham's number 21 pit in Little Neston. The men set gunpowder charges and blew up the road tunnel from Cottingham's number 21 pit and one blast was described as sounding like a cannon. Cottingham took Stanley to court for trespass and damage to the road which caused an estimated production loss of 10 to 12 tons of coal a day with a saleable value of 10 shillings (50p) a ton. Stanley was eventually fined £2,000, a very large sum in those days. Local miners mentioned in court proceedings as witnesses to events were Thomas Roberts, William Jones, Samuel Jones, James Unie, William Lawley, William Swift, William Oxton, Richard Blundell and Joshua Cabry, whose family later ran the *Wheatsheaf* pub in Ness. Thomas Cottingham died four years later.

The method of transporting coal in boats was abandoned, the canals were pumped out and a railway system was laid for waggons called 'tubs', drawn by pit ponies which lived down the mines.

Thomas Stanley's profits were declining and borings were made in 1826 to find fresh coal deposits. John Watson of Mostyn was brought in to assess the situation and suggest ways of making Ness Colliery more efficient. He wrote several letters (2) containing recommendations and accounts.

One letter written by Watson in 1829 recommends several alterations which would cost about £34 or £35, including the use of horses to waggon coals along the seven foot seam instead of waggoning them along the two-foot seam using labourers, thus making a considerable saving.

Another letter written in June 1830 lists the following accounts of Ness Colliery which he discussed with coal agent Mr. Gregory:

```
7th October to 31st December 1829,  coals raised.......2,402 tons.
                                    at a cost of.......£729 - 16 shillings.
31st December to 7th April 1830,    coals raised.......2,945 tons.
                                    at a cost of.......£906 - 17 shillings.
7th April to 2nd June 1830,         coals raised.......1,057 tons.
                                    at a cost of.......£447 - 7 shillings.
Owing for Royalty Rent, timber, other
goods and the keeping of the ponies, at cost of.......£252
                                                      ------
                        Total Expenses.     £2,336 - 1 shilling.
```

```
Amount of coals sold during the above period,........ £2,536 - 1s - 8d pence.
Coal resting on the bank 100 ton,           .............£35.
                                            -------
                  Total value of coals.     £2,571 - 1s - 8 pence.

        Balance in profit to this period,.......£235 - 0s - 8 pence.
```

These figures show that profits were not great. *"Coal resting on the bank"* would have been heaped by the river awaiting shipment to Ireland. The letter goes on to say that the Cottinghams were working close by.

Miners in Wirral, as in every other area, liked a drink. Hard work in a dusty atmosphere gives a man a thirst and ale was looked upon as a tonic and a 'medicine' to swill out their throats. There were plenty of pubs in the Neston area during the 1830s for the miners to choose from:
NESTON.
Bay Horse, Brewers Arms, Black Bull, Coach & Horses, Golden Lion, Greenland Fishery, Hope & Anchor, Nag's Head, Plough, Spotted Cow and the *White Horse*.
LITTLE NESTON.
Bull & Dog, Royal Oak and the *Welch Harp*.
There were also a number of beerhouses and grogshops which people opened in rooms of local cottages where cheap beer was sold. The *Welch Harp*, managed in those days by Robert Robinson, was the most popular pub with the miners as it was the closest to the collieries. Some time later the pub became known as the *Old Harp Inn* and is still standing today. The Earl of Shrewsbury owned most of Little Neston and all of Oxton, in both areas pubs were named the *Shrewsbury Arms* after him.

In the 1830s there was one coal pit in Little Neston and a total of six in Ness, situated in two areas referred to as *Denna Coal Works* and *Snab Pits*. Little Neston mine was at this time owned by Cottingham & Leacroft.

Cottingham & Leacroft's mine and Stanley's Denhall Colliery in Ness were both still working steadily in 1841. At this time there were 24 coal miners and four coal carriers listed as living in Neston. In Little Neston were 30 miners and one agent and in Ness lived 36 miners and a coal agent.

The 1846 tithe map and apportionment of Ness records Charles Stanley as the owner of Denhall Colliery and Limekilns. But the tithe map and apportionments of Little Neston drawn up in 1849 show no working mines in that village. The site of Cottinghams mine is recorded as being owned by the Court of Chancery, which is the Government, and a cottage there was occupied by an Isaac Jackson the coal agent.

The 1851 census records James Gregory of Denhall (who worked for the Stanleys at Ness Colliery) as a 64 year old colliery proprietor employing a total of 120 men. As the number of miners recorded in 1851 was 97, there must have been 23 surface workers including carriers, blacksmiths and clerks etc. This information indicates that only Ness Colliery was working and that Little Neston Colliery was closed at the time.

Nearly half of the miners lived in Ness, 31 lived in Little Neston, 20 in Great Neston and one in Parkgate. Nearly all were born locally. Many were descendants of the men brought in from Wales and Lancashire a century before. They formed a close knit community, particularly in Ness and Little Neston. Their names and birth places are recorded below, from the 1851 census.

```
GREAT NESTON.   * Wales  # Lancashire.
-------------
NAME            AGE     BORN            NAME            AGE     BORN
Anyon Willm.    30      Ness            Jones Joe.      38      Ness
Williams Wm.    31      Neston.
```

PINNINGTONS YARD.
| Bartley Wm. | 16 | | Neston. | Roberts Thos. | 40 | * | Northop. |
| Swift Thos. | 38 | | Ness. | Williams Thos. | 40 | | Neston. |

CHESTER LANE.
Bartley John	14		Neston.	Gleave Geo.	50		Neston.
Gleave Jas.	56		Neston.	Gleave Willm.	52		Neston.
Jones John	30		Neston.	Meessom Hugh	58	*	Harwarden.
Peters Willm.	28		Lt. Neston.	Williams John	28		Neston.
Williams Sam.	70		Neston.				

PEMBERTONS GREEN.   LION YARD.
| Lay William. | 36 | | Burton. | Ball Willm. | 17 | | Burton. |

THE ROCK.
| Roberts Wm. | 49 | | Neston. | Able Robert | 52 | | Neston. |

PARKGATE
| Mellor Thos. | 52 | | Parkgate. | | | | |

NESS.

THE VILLAGE.
Bryan John	46		Ness.	Bryan John	23		Ness.
Bryan Willm.	66		Ness.	Burkey Willm.	26		Ness.
Cartwright John	75		Willaston.	Cartwright Thos.	23		Willaston.
Cartwright Wm.	39		Lt. Neston.	Cottrell Wm.	28		Ness.
Ducker Chas.	16		Ness.	Ducker John	42	*	Ewloe
Eccles Willm.	48	#	St. Helens.	Eccles Willm.	13		Ness.
Jellicoe Edw.	22		Ness.	Jellicoe Thos,	49		Ness.
Jellicoe Thos.	18		Ness.	Jones Willm.	60		Neston.
Lawley Dan.	18		Ness.	Lawley Geo.	25		Ness.
Lawley John	42		Burton.	Lawley Peter	27		Storeton.
Levins Thos.	53		Ireland.	Smith Thos.	46		Lt. Neston.
Williams Dan.	46		Burton.				

NESS HOLT.
Davidson Edw.	47	*	Harwarden.	Jones Edw.	50		Storeton.
Jones John	25		Ness.	Jones Joe.	20		Ness.
Jones Willm.	22		Ness.	Lightfoot Rob.	33		Ness.
Roberts Thos.	39		Ness.	Roberts Thos.	19		Lt. Neston.

NEW HOUSES.
Archer Willm.	44		Ness.	Lewis Rich.	18		Ness.
Lewis John	13		Ness.	Littlemore Thos.	29		Lt. Neston.
Metcalf Stepn.	25	*	Ewloe.	Swift John	50		Ness.
Swift John	19		Ness.				

COLLIERY.
Bryan John	32		Lt. Neston.	Bryan Thos.	56		Ness.
Littlemore Jos.	68		Neston.	Littlemore Jos.	24		Ness.
Newton Isaac	62	*	Ewloe.	Sharp Geo.	22		Ness.
Smith Willm.	23		Ness.				

LITTLE NESTON 1851.

THE VILLAGE.
Able Hugh	18		Ness.	Able Thos.	37		Neston.
Duncan Thos.	16		Lt. Neston.	Duncan Wm.	30		Lt. Neston.
Ellison John	44	*	Harwarden.	Ellison John	16		Lt. Neston.
Hampson Jas.	41		Neston.	Jellicoe Wm.	52		Ness.
Jones Edw.	20		Ness.	Jones Thos.	35		Ness.
Jones Willm.	16		Lt. Neston.	Lawley Thos.	32		Ness.
Littlemore Thos.	68		Neston.	Peers Sam.	33	*	Pentrobine.
Peers Ben.	24	*	Buckley.	Robinson Rich.	56	#	St. Helens.
Smith Miles	23		Lt. Neston.	Smith Thos.	31		Lt. Neston.
Tunstall Thos.	13		Neston.	Williams Edw.	53		Burton.
Williams Thos.	29		Ness.	Woods James	38		Ness.
Woods Peter	9		Lt. Neston	Woods Thos.	11		Lt. Neston.

(Pentrobine is probably Pentrobin Farm, Dobs Hill, Harwarden.)

```
DEE COTTAGES.
Bartley Thos.      18      Neston          Williams Wm.    51      Neston.
ELM COTTAGES.
Peers Thos.        30      Willaston       Roberts Edw.    29      Lt. Neston
Woods Willm.       22      Lt. Neston.
COLLIERY.
Jackson Isaac      45      Lt. Neston (Coal Agent).
Newton Isaac       26   *  Aston, Flintshire.
```

When the census was taken, a sloop called the *Mary* was anchored in the Dee and recorded as *"lying off Ness Colliery"*. The sloop was probably waiting to take coal on board. The master was William Griffiths aged 28 and the mate was 20 year old Thomas Davies, both born in Bagillt.

Although Isaac Jackson of Little Neston Colliery is registered as a coal agent, the mine was not working. He was probably doing safety work on the shafts with Isaac Newton who lived with him and selling coal from stock piles.

The above lists show that at this time the mining community was almost entirely local. Of the 13 men from outside Wirral, 10 came from the nearby Welsh mining areas, two from St. Helens and one from Ireland.

There were a few young lads registered as miners. James Woods and his sons Thomas aged 11 and Peter aged nine were all employed at Ness Colliery. All over Britain children worked long hours in mines. Lord Shaftesbury went down several mines and found children pulling loaded carriages along dark tunnels too narrow for men. He tried to get the working day for children limited to 10 hours but was told by the "powers that be" that it would ruin the country. Eventually, in 1833 Lord Shaftesbury succeeded in having the childrens working hours reduced and instigated the passing of the 1842 Mines and Collieries Act. This Act made it illegal for small children to be employed down mines. However it was not until 1860 that the minimum age for underground workers was raised from 10 years to 12. This was 53 years after slavery had been abolished in Britain.

Seams of different heights and types of coal being worked at Denhall Colliery were seven-foot soft five-quarter, five-foot badger, and the two-foot. In some parts of the two foot seam, it was said that if a man rested his elbow on the floor of the tunnel he could touch the roof with his finger tips. With conditions like that, together with thick black dust, a damp atmosphere and freezing winter weather, it is small wonder so many miners died young. The life expectancy of a Neston coal face miner was far less than that of a negro slave working in the cotton fields of Virginia. Even after working in those terrible conditions these tough men could laugh; when a particularly small miner passed they joked, "he works in the two foot".

All pits were closed by the mid 1850s and Denhall Gutter had silted up, preventing coal boats from reaching *Denhall Quay*. This robbed the collieries of cheap direct transport to their main customers overseas. Having to rely on the poor roads of the day made transporting wagon loads of coal overland slow, difficult, and costly. The loss of shipping facilities together with some seams being worked out caused the closure of both Stanley's mines at Denhall, Ness and Cottinghams of Little Neston. The late Thomas Cottingham's son, Theodore, had also died and it appears that the two surviving sons, John and Thomas, had no more to do with mining. Thomas, a blind retired army Lieutenant on half pay, lived in Little Neston with his Jamaican born wife Sarah.

The above facts are borne out by White's 1860 Directory and the 1861 census. White's 1860 Directory records that; *In Little Neston were formerly some extensive collieries, from which large quantities of coal were exported to Ireland.* The same directory said of Ness, *There were formerly some extensive collieries in this township, which are now in disuse.*

Hewing coal from the mine face.

The 1861 census registers only three miners living in Ness, two in Little Neston and four in Great Neston. This indicates that production had ceased in all mines and these few men were probably employed to maintain various shafts for safety reasons. There were also three miners living in Ness recorded as being "coal miners in Lancashire". This indicates that miners from the Neston area had been been forced to work away from home.

Some time later the colliery yard which had belonged to the Cottingham family was re-opened as a smelting works which was believed to be called the Anglian Smelting Works. This company closed after only a few years.

The local mining industry was still on hard times during the 1870s, as the 1871 census records only five miners in the villages of Great Neston, Ness and Little Neston. One was Richard Robinson of Burton Road, who was then 84, and two others were George and John Lawley who were formerly recorded as being "miners in Lancashire" in 1861. Apart from Neston the only other coal mining area in Cheshire at this time was outside Bollington near Macclesfield at a village called Pott Shrigley.

In 1873 borings were made in Little Neston to locate new stocks of coal. Borings 200 yards deep were made in Heswall two years later, financed by Mr. Bromley Davenport. This exercise was carried out in a field called the *Scouts Meadow* (between Manners Lane and Riverbank Road) but only red rock was brought up. Borings had previously been made in other Wirral villages, including Bidston, Woodchurch, Grange, Meols, Eastham, Little Saughall and Shotwick. At Grange and Eastham the coal was estimated to be only 300 feet down but in Shotwick bunter sandstone was found to be resting on a bed of coal at a depth of 510 feet. There was no doubt that there were seams of coal, which were outcrops of the Flintshire coalfield, running under Wirral. For centuries coal had been mined in counties on both sides of the Wirral peninsula, in Wales and in Lancashire villages from Huyton to Wigan.

The 1874 map of the Ness and Little Neston area shows all the mines disused and the Smelting Works closed down. Fresh borings found worthwhile deposits of coal on the site of the Smelting Works at the bottom of what is today Marshlands Road. During 1876 a new shaft called *King Mine* was sunk close to the River Dee and the colliery was re-named Neston Colliery Company. A railway line was laid connecting the colliery with the main railway network. This rail link gave the colliery a new lease of life. It enabled the railway companies to load coal direct from the colliery and they became the main customers for Neston Colliery Company coal. Seams worked were the seven-foot soft five-quarter, six-foot strong bony king coal, five-foot badger, four-foot, bastard cannel and others. Cannel coal burned with a smokeless flame and was used in the manufacture of coal gas. The seven-foot was the deepest seam, being nearly 500 feet down.

Key men were brought in from outside the area for the skilled and dangerous job of sinking the new shaft. One of these men was my wife's great-grandfather Ellis Roberts who was born in 1854 in the village of Iscoyd, on the Welsh border between Malpas and Whitchurch. During the sinking of the shaft there was a rock fall and the sides caved in, burying some of the men. Luckily no-one was killed but Ellis's leg was badly crushed. He was carried to a nearby house where his leg was amputated on the kitchen table.

Ellis 'Peg-Leg' Roberts with workmates at Wirral Colliery. His peg leg was specially made by the colliery carpenter. Although he was seriously ill after his leg was amputated he eventually made a full recovery and lived to celebrate his diamond wedding anniversary before he died in 1938 aged 84.

After this accident he was no longer fit to go down the mine and for a while he probably wanted to get away from the colliery. When Ellis was fit enough he gained employment on a farm in Neston for a while and also began courting Anne Jellicoe, who was born in Ness but was then living at 15 Cross Street. In 1878 Ellis and Anne were married at St. John the Baptist's Church in Chester and Ellis was registered as a farm worker. Soon he went back to the colliery where he gained employment as a coal carrier or carter, transporting coal in horse-drawn wagons. At this time he and Anne lived in a miner's cottage in the Badgers Butt (later called Badger Bait). Soon after the terraced houses in New Street were built he moved into number 14 and in later years he was employed at the mine as engine man. He often told tales of his boyhood in the villages of Iscoyd, Higher Wychough and Lower Wychough, in the Welsh border area where he was brought up.

King Mine was opened in 1877 using the modern machinery of the day with more efficient pumps. A winding house was built and a new engine installed. It must not have been long before coal from the new pit was being sold throughout Wirral. An entry for 14 November 1878 in the diary of Henry Totty of *Lydiate Farm*, Heswall, says "Very fair coal selling at 8s (40p) per ton at Ness Colliery". In those days people still referred to the mine as Ness Colliery even though by this time the only working mine was actually in Little Neston.

Many of the cottages the miners lived in were hovels but in about 1880 new rows of terraced houses were built in parts of Little Neston mainly for miners brought in from Wales and Lancashire. There were 144 miners living in the local villages. In Great Neston lived 27 miners, in Parkgate two, Ness 19 and Little Neston 96. There were also a number of men employed at the colliery as engine drivers, blacksmiths, joiners and carriers etc. Since the 1850s when the mines were last in full swing the pattern had changed. The majority of miners now lived in Little Neston and not Ness, mainly because the Ness mine was closed and new houses were built close to the new mine in Little Neston.

Many of the men who had last mined when Denhall pits were open 20-odd years before were either dead or had retired, and others had moved or found alternative employment and had decided not to go back to mining. The younger men of the Neston area were in no hurry to become miners. Word of the working conditions and dangers did not encourage local young men to take up the pick as their fathers and grandfathers had done. Still, in those days of work or want, many men from the villages about Neston were forced by poverty to go down the pit. However, because it had been so long since the mines had been in full production, there were not enough experienced colliers, so men from other areas were brought in.

In those days there were scores of small privately owned pits all over the North Wales counties of Flintshire and Denbighshire and also in Lancashire, Yorkshire, Derbyshire and every other mining county. In the Wigan area alone there are 1,013 known shafts in a five mile radius of the town centre and during the 1870s there were over 40 working pits in the area. In all mining counties old shafts were worked out and closed and new ones opened on a regular basis. There was a constant shift in labour from pit to pit, much the same as building workers moved from site to site a few decades ago.

News of pits needing men was often carried to mining villages by railway workers. The new railway networks enabled miners seeking work to travel to various mining districts with ease, something which, in their grandfathers day, would have been a major trek.

During the 1880s just over half the colliers living in the old mining hamlet of Denhall in Ness were born and bred locally. But in Great Neston over half the miners were born outside Wirral and in Little Neston the figure was over three-quarters. In some mining neighbourhoods of Little Neston there were hardly any locals. Many of these miners had lived and worked in coal fields in various parts of Wales and the North of England. This is to be seen in the recorded birth places of their wives and children. Some of the young single miners from outside Wirral married and stayed in the Neston area.

From the 1700s there was a steady flow of people from outside Wirral into the Neston area seeking work. A good many were from Ireland, Wales and Lancashire. This sudden influx of a large number of miners and their families during the 1870s and 1880s further broadened the already distinct West Wirral accent, enriching it with more dialect words and phrases.

Below are the ages and birth places of miners and colliery employees recorded in the census taken on 4 April 1881.

GREAT NESTON.

PINNINGTONS YARD.   * Wales   # Lancashire   + Yorkshire   = Staffordshire.

NAME	AGE		BORN	NAME	AGE		BORN
Aston Thos.	35	*	Jobs Hill.	Blundell John	26	#	Liverpool.
Jones Willm.	32	*	Flintshire.	Peters Joe.	18		Lt. Neston.

(Jobs Hill is probably Dobs Hill).

BRIDGE STREET.

NAME	AGE		BORN	NAME	AGE		BORN
Bentley John	56		Neston.	Cottrell Rob.	30		Neston.
Jones Owen	48	*	Hope.	Lewis Rich.	21	#	Wigan.
McDonald Jas.	26		Dublin Ir.	Parkins Ben.	31	=	Ashley.
Riley Thos.	25		Ireland.	Taylor Thos.	35		Lt. Neston.

MILL STREET.

NAME	AGE		BORN	NAME	AGE		BORN
Anyon Thos.	24		Neston.	Bartley Willm.	46		Neston.
Comer Chas.	22	*	Buckley.	Jones Chris.	19		Neston.
Millin Thos.	22	*	Buckley.	Millington Wm.	23	*	Brymbo.
Roberts Thos.	27		Cornwall.	Rutter Willm.	20		Neston.

LIVERPOOL ROAD.

NAME	AGE		BORN	NAME	AGE		BORN
Booth Jas.	29	#	Haywood.	Evans Lambert	19	#	Manchester.
Mathews Rob.	21		Sutton.	Redfern Rich.	40	*	Flint.
Roberts John	45	*	Anglesey.	Williams Hugh	54	*	Mostyn.
Williams Wm.	22	*	Flint.				

PARKGATE.

NAME	AGE		BORN	NAME	AGE		BORN
Norman Geo.	34		Parkgate.	Peers Thos.	61		Willaston.

NESS.

DENHALL.

NAME	AGE		BORN	NAME	AGE		BORN
Carrington Rob.	26	*	Wales.	Cottrell Thos.	54		Ness.
Cottrell Wm.	60		Ness.	Davies John	21	*	Wales.
Hailshouse Wm.	74		Ness.	Hughes Joe.	17	*	Wales.
Hughes Thos.	48	*	Wales.	Jellicoe Edw.	52		Ness.
Jellicoe Jas.	52		Ness.	Jones John	15	*	Wales.
Jones Willm.	48		Ness.	Lawley Geo.	55		Ness.
Parr Rich.	59		Puddington.	Sharps Willm.	17		Stockport.
Sharps Geo.	27		Ness.	Thomas Sam.	34	*	Wales.
Tyson Geo.	24	*	Wales.	Williams Wm.	32		Lt. Neston.
Williams Wm.	21		Ness.				

LITTLE NESTON.

NEWTOWN.

NAME	AGE		BORN	NAME	AGE		BORN
Corless John	23		Ireland.	Evans Ralph	23	*	Mold.
Evans Thos.	51	*	Mold.				

DEE COTTAGES.

NAME	AGE		BORN	NAME	AGE		BORN
Bennett Moses	25	#	Wigan.	MacDonald Andrew	28		Kildare Ir.

BADGER BUTT.

NAME	AGE		BORN	NAME	AGE		BORN
Bell George	16		Neston.	Dennit Thos.	30	#	Wigan.
Edwards Jas.	22	*	Buckley.	Evans John	33	*	Northop.
Evans Thos.	28	*	Mold.	Jones Geo.	21	*	Aston.
Jones Willm.	36	*	Aston.	Kirkum Wm.	50	*	Denbighshr.
Lawley Jas.	62		Ness.	Lawley John	18		Lt. Neston.
Lawley Joe.	24		Neston.	Lewis Peter	28	*	Buckley.
McGowan Rich.	15	*	Buckley.	Millitt Joe	14		Lt. Neston.
Price Thos.	31	*	Ewloe.	Roberts Ellis	26		Malpas.
Shone Thos.	28	*	Buckley.	Thornton John	22	#	St. Helens.

It has been said that the cottages in the Badger Butt (later re-named Badger Bait) took their name from one of the seams being mined at the time, the five-foot badger.

TOWN LANE.

NAME	AGE		BORN
Leadbetter Jas.	27		Neston.

VICTORIA ROAD.

Becket Jas.	31		Hampshire.	Hart Chas.	32		Northants.
Peers Sam.	21	*	Harwarden.	Ramsden J. F.	42	#	Oldham.

(James Fletcher Ramsden was the Colliery Manager).

THE VILLAGE.

Jones Edw.	24	*	Ewloe.	Jones Isaac	41	*	Dublin Fl.
Lawley Joe.	29		Neston.	Lewis Jas.	18		Neston.
Lewis Rich.	47		Lt. Neston.	Murray Chris.	16		Lt. Neston.
Murray Rich.	14		Lt. Neston.	Oliver John	22	=	Kidsgrove.
Oxton Jas.	18		Lt. Neston.	Oxton Joe.	18		Lt. Neston.
Oxton Willm.	21		Lt. Neston.	Roberts Robt.	25	*	L. Dublin
Roscoe Dan.	20		Lt. Neston.	Roscoe Thos.	30		Lt. Neston.
Swift Joe.	35		Ness.	Wellings Harry	30	*	Montgomery.
Williams Joe.	25		Bromborough	Williams John	54		Neston.

Below is the community known collectively as *The Colliery* at the bottom of Wood Lane, later called Colliery Lane, now Marshlands Road. In this neighbourhood in 1881 only one miner was born in the Neston area, and most were from Wales and Lancashire. Even the *Harp Inn* and *Colliery Farm* had miners lodging there. *Colliery Row*, later called *Seven Row* because it was a terrace of seven cottages, had only just been built, in fact one house was uninhabited and was probably not finished. *Sea View Cottages,* later called *New Street,* because that is exactly what it was, was still being built. When completed, New Street consisted of a terrace of 21 houses on one side and 18 on the other, as it still is today. At the time of the 1881 census only the side with 21 houses was completed. Many mining families had miners lodging with them.

COLLIERY.

Brown Thos.	22		Wolverhptn.	Dowell Willm.	39	*	Prestatyn.
Jones John	26		Chester.	Jones Robt.	33	*	Prestatyn.
Kendrick Ishmail	15		Lt. Neston.				

HARP INN.   COLLIERY FARM.

Wragg John	71	+	Sheffield	Molyneaux Wm.	23	#	Wigan.

COLLIERY ROW, numbers 1 to 7.

1.	Barnes Geo.	31		Nth. of Eng.	2. Whittington R.	40	#	Liverpool.
3.	Davies Geo.	48	*	Hope.	4. Hodson Peter	40	#	Shevington.
	Davies Seth	17	*	Tryddyn.	6. Uninhabited.			
	Peers John	25	*	Northop.	7. Hilling Thos.	21	*	Ridgeway.
5.	Richardson J.	60	*	Whitford.	Hilling Wm.	25	*	Ridgeway.
	Richardson J.	21	*	Whitford.	Letman Edw.	20	*	Harwarden.
	Jones John	21	*	Whitford.	Parrish Abram	57	*	Greenfield.
	Roberts Eli	28	*	Whitford.				

(Ridgeway is recorded as being in Pembrokeshire).

WOOD LANE.

Eatock Rich.	52	#	Wigan.	Peers Thos.	23	*	Harwarden.

SEA VIEW COTTAGES, numbers 1 to 21.

1.	James Evan	45		Pontesbury.	12. Tickle Peter	33	*	Pemberton.
	Bennett Ben.	19	*	Llanarden.	13. Millington W.	34	*	Buckley.
2.	Gorgeson Ed.	55	#	Aughton.	14. Golding Thos.	34	#	Pemberton.
3.	Jones Dan.	23	*	Mold.	15. Kevan Anthy.	28		S. Tranmere
4.	Prescott Jn.	27	#	Hindley.	16. Davidson Frk.	39	*	Buckley.
5.	Pickles Hry.	28	#	Wigan.	Davidson Geo.	15	*	Ewloe.
	Pickles Thos.	67	+	Hevensill	17. Beattie Wm.	34	#	Wigan.
	Lloyd Thos.	37	*	Harwarden	Grimes Thos.	19	#	Wigan.
6.	Wilson Hry.	39	#	Orrel.	Hughes Edw.	19	*	Dublin Fl.
	Wilson John	17	#	Wigan.	18. Lamb Willm.	28	*	Buckley.
7.	Fowler Jas.	32	+	Ripon.	Lewis Willm.	30	*	Buckley.
	Handley Wm.	32		Neston.	Morris Peter	28	*	Buckley.
8.	Eatock Isaac	28	#	Wigan.	Burrows Jas.	30	#	St. Helens.
	Cross Willm.	23	#	Wigan	Neil Henry	18		Stapple Fo.

```
9.  Hilton Thos.   37  #  St. Helens.    19. Uninhabited.
10. Hughes Joe.    48  *  Northop.       20. Westhead Wm.  27  #  Hindley.
    Hughes Dan.    16  *  Northop            Bradley Wm.   50  *  Ruabon.
    Hughes Joe.    14  *  Northop.       21. Aspinall Wm.  38  #  St. Helens
11. Hampson Hry.   30  #  Aspell.            Crooks Thos.  21  #  Wigan.
                                             Tabern Peter  22  #  Wigan.
```

Only Ishmail Kendrick, William Handley the colliery carpenter and the shop-keeper Anthony Kevan, who was a baker and grocer from South Tranmere, were born in Wirral. The mine owners brought Anthony in to supply bread and groceries for the new community. Other men employed in the colliery at tasks other than mining were Daniel Jones the coal mine engine driver, Richard Whittington the stoker, William Westhead the mine fireman and Henry Wilson and his nephew John were pick sharpeners.

Jane Thomas, a widow from Mold was the tenant of number seven Colliery Row who made a living by taking in four Welsh miners as lodgers. The miners listed as being from Little Dublin and Dublin, Flintshire were from a hamlet of Northop Hall which was so called because Irish miners and railway workers settled there. The Welsh name for Northop Hall is Pentre Moch which means "Village of the Pigs".

Mines in the Neston area were always wet and prone to flooding. Water was constantly seeping down into the tunnels from the River Dee above and pumps had to be working night and day to keep the water level down. Sometimes the miners were flooded out and laid off work, which led to many leaving the area. In the 1880s there was a particularly bad flood when several pit ponies were drowned and their carcasses had to be got out and disposed of.

Flooding was not the only danger, as in any mine there were the dangers of poison gas and rock falls. The invention of the Davy safety lamp considerably lessened the chance of gas explosions and also if methane was present the flame inside the lamp grew brighter. Colliers still took cage birds down the mine and kept them close by. They were the gas early warning back-up system. A whiff of poisonous gas and the bird fell off the perch. It was also said that if the pit ponies smelt gas they became restless and started to whinny. The danger of poison gas is highlighted by two deaths recorded in Neston Church a century earlier. It appears that vagrants dossed down in some of the old tunnels and workings as, on 5 May 1790, the deaths of two paupers, James Glaves and Edward Davies were recorded as *suffocated in coal pits*. This probably meant that they were overcome by fumes.

In Neston Churchyard are graves of some of the men killed at Neston Colliery including Isaac Fisher aged 66 killed in 1876 and Edwin Hooson aged 47 killed in 1882. One of the biggest dangers was solid fossilised trees in the coal seams. The miners cut through them but sometimes a tree might suddenly drop down into the tunnel on top of men working.

As in any industry, particularly one as hard as mining, workers came and went. To some men brought up to it, mining was their chosen profession, to others it was the best paid job they could get, or a short-term stop-gap.

In 1884 the miners went on strike for better pay. This caused the closing of the Neston Colliery Company. It eventually re-opened under the name of Wirral Colliery Company.

The census of 1891 records 153 mine employees, the same as 10 years earlier. However there was a shift in personnel from the previous 10 years. Although there were still a great number of miners from outside Wirral, in 1891 there were far more local men employed at the colliery, nearly twice as many as 10 years before. This was due to many miners being forced to return to Lancashire and Wales when the colliery closed. Poor conditions which affected their wages also caused miners from other areas, particularly single men, to move back home when news of available work reached them. With miners wages depending on production bonuses, flooding or a seam of hard coal slowed them down and cost them money.

Below is a list of mine workers and places of birth from the census taken 6 April 1891.

```
GREAT NESTON.           * Wales  # Lancashire  + Yorkshire  = Staffordshire.
-------------
NAME                AGE     BORN                NAME                AGE     BORN
PYKES WEINT.                                    BIRCHES WEINT.
Coventry Wm.        21      Neston.             Parry Thos.         28  *  Mold.
HARDY'S WEINT.                                  CHESTER ROAD.
Jones Willm.        34      Neston.             Bartley Joe.        25     Neston.
GAS WORKS.                                      PARKGATE ROAD.
Clarke Joe.         16      Stretton.           Jones Arthur        48  *  Bistre.
PINNINGTONS YARD.
Jones Chris.        34      Neston.             Ollerhead John      16     Neston.
Williams Thos.      37  *   Holywell.
HIGH STREET.
Garnham Willm.      46      Suffolk.            Hughes Willm.       35  *  Flint.
Mawdsley Rich.      32  #   Skelmersdale.       Williams Hugh       47  *  Mostyn.
Bell William        21      Parkgate.
PEAR TREE CRESCENT.
Taylor Thos.        37      Lt. Neston.         Williams Edw.       19     Neston.
Williams Wm.        13      Neston.
GLADSTONE ROAD.
Scarratt Steph.     34      Neston.             Johnson Thos.       20     Lt. Neston.
Evans Job           54  *   Halkin.             Evans Willm.        20  *  Mostyn.
BRIDGE STREET.
Bartley Thos.       42      Neston.             Bennett Ben.        29  *  Buckley.
Blackwell John      25  *   Rhossmore.          Johnson John        28     Neston.
ELDON TERRACE.
Blackwell Joe.      27  *   Kyouse.             Leadbetter Jas.     36     Neston.
Leadbetter Joe.     18  #   Billinge.           Johnson Wm.         24     Neston.
Jones John          69      Ness.               Jones John          26  #  Rainford.
Jones Edwin         21  #   Rainford.           Jones Willm.        37     Neston.
Smith Willm.        15      Neston.             Williams John       29     Neston.
Williams Sam.       21      Neston.             Wheeler Joe.        21     Neston.
(Kyouse was probably meant to be Caerwis).
MILL STREET.
Anyon Fredrk.       24      Neston.             Anyon Thos.         33     Neston.
Brournsworth Geo.   21      Neston.             Evans Robt.         22  *  Flintshire.
Lewis Rich.         32  #   Wigan.              Medcalf Joe.        36  *  Flintshire.
Price Geo.          26      Neston.             Rugman Wm.          31     Kingston.
Roberts George      52      Ness Holt.
LIVERPOOL ROAD.
Brieman Mich.       68      Armagh Ir.          Cayless Joe.        25     Leicester.
Davies James        24      Heswall.            Ellis Mark          30     Heswall.
Evans Lambert       29  #   Manchester.         Meadows Jas.        33     Neston.
Mealor John         33      Neston.             Mealor Will.        17     Neston.
Price Edw.          29      Neston.
CROSS STREET.
Blundell John       37      Neston.             Briscoe Thos.       20     Scotland.
PARKGATE.
Norman George       44      Neston.             Norman John         20  #  Rainford.
Norman George       18  #   Bickerstaff.        Oxton William       30     Neston.

LEIGHTON.
---------
Duckers John        20      Neston.

LITTLE NESTON.
--------------
Able Fredrk.        18      Neston.             Able William        15     Neston.
Anyon Joe.          24      Neston.             Aspinall Wm.        48  #  St. Helens.
```

Curry John	23		O.T.O.N.A.	Daniels John	36	Kent.
Devaney Frank	17	=	Staffs.	Gittins Wm.	20	Ness.
Hampson Henry	40	#	Blackrood.	Hare William	37	* St. Hassell
Hare William	15	*	St. Hassells.	Hughes Joe.	27	* Baghilt.
Hughes Joe.	42	*	Mostyn.	Hughes Thos.	16	* Baghilt.
Jackson Thos.	56		Neston.	Jones Edw.	28	* Harwarden.
Jones James	22		Neston.	Jones John	26	* Flint.
Jones Joe.	51		Neston.	Jones Matt.	19	Lt. Neston.
Jones Owen	56	*	Hope.	Jones Willm.	20	* Pentre.
Jones Arthur	17	*	Pentre.	Jones Peter	36	Bromborough
Jones Peter	31	*	Harwarden.	Jones Peter	30	Chester.
Jones Willm.	40	*	Baghilt.	Lawley James	66	Ness.
Lawley James	36		Neston.	Lawley Joe.	21	# Rainford.
Lawley Willm.	16	#	Rainford.	Lee William	42	High Wycom.
Lewis James	35	*	Flintshire.	Lewis Rich.	58	Neston.
MacFarlane Frc.	32	#	Liverpool.	McIvor Walter	23	Ruston Ch.
Millet Joe.	23		Lt. Neston.	Millet Geo.	16	Lt. Neston.
Millington Ellis	27	*	Aston.	Millington Geo.	29	* Buckley.
Millington Thos.	38	*	Buckley.	Millington Wm.	30	* Northop.
Moors George	21		Neston.	Morris Sam.	27	* Connahs Qu.
Oxton Alfred	18		Lt. Neston.	Oxton George	22	Lt. Neston.
Oxton Joe.	20		Lt. Neston.	Parry Isaac	23	* Flintshire.
Peers Henry	23		Neston.	Peers Willm.	15	Neston.
Platt James	47	#	St. Helens	Platt John	23	# Bickerstaff
Price Thos.	40	*	Harwarden.	Quigley Thos.	17	Lt. Neston.
Roberts Ellis	35		Malpas.	Robinson Jas.	52	Eamont. Br.
Robinson John	18		Lt. Neston.	Roscoe Absolem	28	Neston.
Smith Joe.	26		Neston.	Smith John	21	Neston.
Smith George	16		Lt. Neston.	Smith Joe	16	Neston.
Sharp Joseph	14		Neston.	Tudor Joe.	23	* Wrexham.
Tudor Robt.	63	#	Chorley.	Tyra Rich.	40	# Hindley.
Wheller Wm.	26		Neston.	Wilke William	50	Ness.
Williams Joe.	28	*	Northop.	Williams Wm.	40	* Holyhead.
Wright George	30	*	Aston.	Wynne John	33	* Newmarket.

(James Platt was the colliery manager).

NESS.

Bailey Henry	38	=	Burslem.	Beattie Geo.	19	Neston.
Beattie James	24		Ness.	Jones Edw.	34	* Harwarden.
Jones Geo.	29	*	Harwarden.	Jones Charles	30	# Billinge.
Lawley Geo.	30		Ness.	Lawley Geo.	64	Ness.
McDonald James	30	=	Staffs.	Parking Thos.	21	* Buckley.
Phillips Horace	26		Cambridge.	Wilde James	37	Ness.

NESS HOLT.

Jones Edw.	33	#	Billington.	Jones William	60	Neston.
Jones Thos.	19	*	Flint.	Jones Willm.	21	* Flint.

NESS COLLIERY.

Jellicoe Thos.	20		Neston.	Thomas Sam.	44	* Wales.
Williams Wm.	27		Neston.			

Some of the local born families listed above had been working in the pits for many generations. The name Anyon is probably the oldest surviving Neston name; I have seen it in documents from the 1500s. As far as I know, Thomas Briscoe is the only miner who worked at Wirral Colliery recorded as being from Scotland.

Quite a few men listed in the 1880s and 1890s had been able to keep in employment by moving to and from various mining areas by rail. Some had married their wives and fathered their children in several different mining towns. A few examples are Frederick Davidson from Buckley, whose wife Amey was from Wigan and his children were born in Ewloe, Sandycroft and Buckley. Frederick is not mentioned in the 1891 census so he and his family must have moved to greener pastures yet again.

Ellen, the wife of George Norman from Parkgate was from Newton-le-Willows and their sons were born in Rainford and Bickerstaff. Job Evans from Halkyn married Ann from Little Neston and his son William was born in Mostyn which means he probably worked in the Little Neston mine at least twice. John Jones aged 69 was born in Ness, his wife Catherine was born in Flint and his sons John and Edwin were born in Rainford. William Wheller had mined furthest away from his home town of Neston, his wife Elizabeth was from Newcastle upon Tyne. Although there are many families in Neston whose ancestors were Welsh and Lancashire miners, there are also families in Bagillt, Wrexham etc. and the Wigan area whose ancestors were from Neston.

Nearly all Welsh miners recorded in Neston were from North Wales but William Hare was born in St. Hassells, Pembrokeshire in South Wales. The birth-places of a couple of men were quite unusual; William Rugman was born in Kingston, North America and John Curry is recorded as having been born on the ocean near Aden.

The area referred to as Ness Holt was called Ness Out by the locals and this spelling is seen on old maps. Ness Out is probably Cheshire dialect for Ness Holt. Holt is an Anglo-Saxon word meaning wood.

Obviously nearly all the men listed above were miners but one or two were employed under different headings. Frances MacFarlane was the colliery lampman, William Wilke colliery horse keeper, Richard Tyra colliery engine tender, William Lee the stationary engine stoker, Ellis Roberts a coal carrier and George Millington the colliery fireman.

Some families which still survive in the area today had sons working in both the traditional local industries of fishing and mining. These included Evans, Jones, Lewis, Mealor, Mellor and Peers. Margaret Peers a widow from Little Neston had four sons, two were miners and two were fishermen. Christopher Jones Senior had worked as a fisherman and young Christopher was a miner. Today, Chris Jones, a descendant of this very old Neston family works as an industrial papermaker and lives in Marlston Avenue, Irby with his wife and children. Jim Mealor, another descendant of one of these old families became a farm bailiff at *Top House Farm* on the Arrowe Estate. Jim now lives at *Arrowe Park*, Barnawatha, Northern Victoria in Australia with his wife Marjorie, nee Wade of Irby and their six children and 10 grandchildren.

During the 1890s the four most popular pubs for miners on their way home were the nearby *Old Harp Inn* run by Sheffield born mariner John Palfreyman, and three Birkenhead Brewery owned pubs, the *Bull and Dog* at Bull Hill, managed by Matthew Roberts and two in Little Neston village, the *Royal Oak* run by William Burkey and the *Durham Ox*, tenant Robert Ostle. There were also 12 pubs in Great Neston and the *Wheatsheaf* in Ness run by John Green.

The 1899 map shows the old pits of Denhall Colliery closed and Wirral Colliery with two shafts still working. Production and workforce figures at the Colliery were up and down during the early 1900s. The quality of the coal was rather poor and the mine was struggling to make a profit. It became apparent that closure was very much a possibility and in 1911 Wirral Colliery went bankrupt but soon re-opened.

The 1912 map shows the Denhall Colliery pits still disused and the two Wirral Colliery pits working. In 1914, the year the Great War started, the colliery was in financial difficulty and closed. It was re-opened in 1915 and re-named Wirral Colliery (1915) Limited. In 1916 the colliery was taken over by the Government. Many of the pit ponies were turned out to grass and replaced by more modern machinery to increase production for the war effort. A number of miners volunteered for military service and altogether 91 men from Neston were killed in the Great War.

As always the colliery was a dangerous and hazardous place, not only below ground but also on the surface. In 1917 my wife's grandfather's 17 year old brother Richard, a former Boy's Brigade Lance Corporal and a member of the junior Neston Volunteer Force, was due to be called up on his 18th birthday on 13 March. Richard, or Dick as he was called, was a surface worker at Wirral Colliery where his father and brothers also worked. On 6 March, as on any other day, Dick's mother brought his mid-day meal to him from their cottage in nearby New Street. When he saw her comming she ran to meet her. Dick slipped on frosty ground and fell under the wheels of the colliery steam train and was killed. His mother was terror-stricken and her hair turned white overnight.

Since leaving school Dick had worked at Wirral Colliery where he was a very popular lad. Hundreds attended his funeral at the church of St. Mary and St. Helen where tribute was paid to him by a guard of honour of the Neston Boy's Brigade.

In 1919, the year after the war ended, the mine was given back to Wirral Colliery (1915) Ltd. which just about managed to keep its head above water. The colliery carried on producing coal of poor quality, but it was only a matter of time before the only pit in Wirral would close.

Life was just as hard for miners in the 1920s, particularly in the cold of winter when they hardly saw daylight for months on end. Working conditions were atrocious; damp, dust and vermin caused a regular turnover of personnel. There were no dust masks or goggles supplied in those days and many a man must have choked in the dust and been half blinded by chips of coal flying from picks and compressed air drills. Some went blind and young deaths were as common as ever.

Years ago, keeping pit ponies down mines led to the harbouring of mice. The mice got down mines in bales of hay and straw. They lived on oats which were fed to the ponies and if miners left their 'carry outs' in coat pockets while they worked, the mice ate them. The only way to stop these unwanted dinner guests was for miners to put their food in tin boxes with lids that snapped shut. The words snap-tin became 'snappin', and that was what the miners of North Wales and Lancashire called their meal breaks. Even today many older Nestoners call lunch 'snappin'.

The odd miner moved away from the Neston area and travelled to the colliery by rail or on push bikes. One such miner was George Anyon who moved to Heswall where, in 1921, aged 21, he married Winifred Apton at St. Peters Church, Heswall.

The Colliery Yearbook and Trades Directory for 1926 records Wirral Colliery director being W.R. Davies of *Errington Lodge*, Aigburth, Liverpool. The seams being worked were the six-foot and seven-foot, producing household, steam and manufacturing coal using compressed air power. The number of employees was more or less the same as it had been in 1881, a total of 148, with 111 working underground and 37 on the surface.

Every year there were a number of accidents at the colliery, in one rock fall George 'Kydo' Jones and several others were injured. When 'Kydo' eventually came out of Chester Infirmary after losing part of his thigh and two fingers, he refused to go back down the pit and became a shepherd on Burton Marsh.

The year 1926 was a particularly bad one for the Neston miners. Frederick Abel aged 24 was killed on 22 January, the last miner to lose his life at Wirral Colliery. There was also a long and bitter strike when mine owners tried to force all miners to accept a cut in pay and work longer hours.

In May 1926 all miners including those in Neston took part in the general strike and stayed out. There was great suffering and poverty. Some miners kept poultry and one or two pigs in the back yard which they either sold or killed and shared out. They also went poaching, rabbiting, wildfowling and fishing and did anything to make a few bob. Mrs. Cissey Evans, a fisherman's widow of Heswall, recalls as a little girl helping her father 'Ginger' Smith pick coal from the slag heaps to heat their home in nearby New Street.

Arthur Bulley, a wealthy Liverpool cotton broker, conservationist and strong socialist who lived at *Mickwell Brow* (the grounds of which were given to Liverpool University and became Ness Gardens) arranged for the miners' families to be provided with food, right through the strike. However after six months of severe hardship the miners had to throw the towel in. They were forced to return to work for less pay, five shillings and eight pence per day (29p) plus bonus.

Wirral Colliery resumed production for a few months but was found to be running at a loss and in 1927 it was decided to reduce the workforce to 60 men and boys and work only the most economical seams. Even with this drastic action, a profit could not be made. The mine was played out and Wirral Colliery (1915) Ltd. gave up the ghost. High production costs, poor quality coal, royalties paid to landowners and a failed bid to buy rights to mine a new coal seam under local farmland, all helped cause the closure of the mine in 1927.

A notice was posted outside the pit giving the men 14 days notice of the closing of the colliery. The notice read: *To all persons employed at the Wirral Colliery. It has now been finally decided to close the pit and dismantle it, therefore 14 days notice expiring March 12th 1927 is hereby given to each person employed.- (signed) John Taylor, manager.*

As a last resort attention was turned to the old Denhall Colliery which had been closed since about 1855. An old pit, situated close to Denhall Quay, was re-opened. This historic last ditch attempt to keep mining alive in the Neston area was witnessed by Bill Williams. Bill recalls two crews going down the derelict shaft, one headed by Henry Williams of *Seven Row* and the other by Jack 'Wrexham' Jones of *Pritchards Row* in Little Neston Village. They were lowered down by a steam winch, mounted and bolted down on the back of a Sentinel steam wagon.

The canals were still down there, with arches cut through the coal. Some of the coal baskets and tubs were still there as well as miner's personal marking tags. Coal of doubtful quality was brought up for a short while before Ness and Little Neston mines were finally abandoned in 1928. The shafts were sealed off, equipment removed and the big shire horses which delivered household coal were sold. A stillness and a feeling of sadness fell over the colliery area.

Although conditions down the pit were appalling it was a sad day for many when the colliery closed. To some men mining was not just a job but a way of life. Whole families were brought up to it and although the work was extremely hard there was a certain comradeship between them. On any job which is a hard struggle and where everyone is in the same boat, there is always camaraderie.

The mines had closed and re-opened many times, but this time the closure was final. A lot of families were put on the bread-line as the pit was Neston's biggest employer. Some miners found alternative employment. A few managed to get jobs at John Summers Steel Works and travelled to Shotton by train or push bike. Some, although out of work would not dream of leaving the village they were brought up in. Others did, and moved to Birkenhead and other areas of Wirral. 'Ginger' Smith went to live in the old Woodchurch Village and became a building worker. Several, such as Bob Peers moved to the mining areas of Buckley and Wrexham to carry on their trade.

One family who moved were the Peters' and unfortunately the move ended in tragedy. The Peters family lived in one of an old row of five sandstone cottages and a shop called *Sebastapool*, which once stood by the green in Little Neston Village. Some time after the mine closed they moved to the Wrexham area and worked at Gresford Colliery. On 22 September

1934 there was a terrible disaster at the mine and 266 men lost their lives, including, I am told, Mr. Peters and his two sons.

The last shift at Wirral Colliery. From left to right; Arthur Jones, Dave Parry, Joe Burkey, Joe Millington, Bill Williams, Riche Williams, John M. Williams, Jack Campion, Henry Williams, and 'Cobber' Jim Jones.

It was a great blow to my wife's great-grandfather, Ellis 'Peg Leg' Roberts, and his sons when the pit shut. Ellis's sons, young Ellis and Ted, my wife's grandfather, had been at Wirral Colliery all their working lives. Ted was in charge of the pit ponies until they were "pensioned off" and Ellis worked in the winding room. Ted caught pneumonia down the pit and luckily found alternative work at Lever Brothers in Port Sunlight before the pit shut down. He used to walk the width of Wirral twice a day, all the way from Seven Row, by the Dee to Port Sunlight near the Mersey. Later he and his wife and 10 children managed to find a house in Buffs Lane off Barnston Road which shortened his walk a bit. As an old man he enjoyed a few pints in the *Sandon Arms* and a well earned retirement in his cottage *The Beeches*, on Telegraph Road, where he often played his penny whistle by the fire-side and sang his favourite song "Danny Boy".

Life was very hard during the 1920s and a good account of it is given by Bill Williams of Ness. The mining families living close to the colliery, in Colliery Lane and Denhall, were a tight knit community during the 1920s. All the families in the *New Street, Seven Row* and *Jacksons Row* area of Little Neston and those in the scattered cottages of Denhall and *New Houses* in Well Lane, knew one another.

Bill was born in *Denhall Farm Cottage* close to the River Dee in the heart of the old mining community. His great grandfather, John Williams from Flintshire, was coachman to the Stanley family. John was a widower and he and Isaac Parry lodged in Little Neston at William Bull's house. Bill's grandfather Joseph Williams was a colliery overlooker; today he would be called a chargehand. Joseph was born in the Welsh mining area of Northop, Flintshire and his wife Mary was born at Ince, Lancashire to Irish parents. Joseph worked in the Little Neston mine from the 1880s until the 1920s, apart from a short break in 1914 when the pit closed and he worked as a postman. Joseph took bad, he was examined by the local doctor and tests were made. Some time later he was sitting talking to friends on a bank known as *The Brew* when the doctor drew up in his car and told him he had cancer. Before very long the colliery management got to know about Joseph's state of health. Within days he got a letter of dismissal saying that the company was sorry to hear about his illness, but he was now considered unfit for mining .

Denhall Farm Cottage, like all the other cottages in Denhall, had no running water and the Williams family, along with many more, relied on a nearby well for fresh water. The well was big and ancient and had probably served the old cottages with water for centuries. There was no bucket pulley like most wells had, but sandstone steps leading down to the water. Bill Williams recalled that in bad weather, mud from peoples' shoes dropped in the water and clouded it so they sometimes went to Jacksons Row for water.

The five cottages in *Jacksons Row* were supplied with running water from an outside tap. Denhall, being part of Ness, came under the jurisdiction of Wirral Urban District Council, whilst the miners' cottages in *Jacksons Row*, a few yards away were in Little Neston and came under the control of Neston Council. Neston Council got to know that families from Ness were using Little Neston water. To put a stop to this, Neston Council had a wooden box built over the tap, with a lock on it and a key for each family in *Jacksons Row*. That night, after a hard day's work, Bill's teenage brother Joe, went to *Jacksons Row* tap for a wash, only to find it locked up. He went home rather annoyed, took an axe and chopped the box up, then washed himself.

During the 1920s the old retired pit ponies still grazed opposite New Street in the *Magazine Field*, so called because at the far end of the field was a brick building where gunpowder was stored. The gunpowder was used by shotfirers Messrs. Carrol and Francis for blasting out the coal. Bill Williams tells me that he and all the other local kids were warned to keep well clear of the gunpowder building when playing out.

During the last few years in which Wirral Colliery struggled to stay open the families of miners whose names we still hear today lived in cottages close to the colliery.
NEW STREET; Barnes, Belton, Hughes, Johnson, Jones, Kerrigan, Lewis, Millington, Monaghan, Price, Roberts, Smith, Tudor, Wynne and Young.
JACKSONS ROW; Harrison, Hare, Jones, Johnson and Woolley.
SEVEN ROW; Carr, Campion, Hare, Jones, Roberts, Sharp and Williams.

The terraced cottages were not really big enough for the large families which many people had in those days. My father-in-law tells me that as a child in *Seven Row* he and his 10 brothers and sisters were terribly cramped. Their neighbours, the Campion's, only had a small family and kindly allowed some of his older brothers to sleep in their house. This gesture shows how communities pulled together in those hard times. The Campion's were another old family employed in both traditional industries, as their relations were Parkgate fishermen.

Many miners had nicknames, partly due to the Neston sense of humour and partly because so many had the same Welsh surnames. Examples were 'Kydo' Jones, 'Wrexham' Jones, 'Cobber' Jones, 'Coachy' Williams and 'Doggy' Williams etc.

Bill William's family were the 'Coachy' Williams' because his great grandad had been a coachman. Bill tells me that many of the miners had hobbies or pastimes which in those hard days either put food on the table or made them a few bob. Several men were bird catchers. They caught linnets and finches by spreading a sticky substance called bird lime on tree branches. These colourful song-birds were then sold as cage-birds. Others fished or trod fluke in the gutters or 'jobbed' them with long shafted forks. Some went across the marsh to set nets in the main channel and were sometimes lucky enough to catch salmon. A lot of miners went rabbiting or wildfowling on the marsh with dog and gun. In those days every family had a shotgun, and geese and duck were sometimes shot from back gardens and yards of cottages near the marsh when flocks flew low on foggy mornings.

A few miners had more unusual hobbies. Gilbert Molyneaux of *Sunset Cottages* in Ness, fixed watches and Dan Jones gathered herbs from the hedges to make ointments. Dan's ointments were much valued by many of the community in those days before the National Health Service, when doctors had to be paid cash.

During the the Second World War sons and grandsons of these tough Neston miners were called upon to defend our nation from the Nazis. Alfred, Cecil, Levi, Eric and John Roberts, sons of Ted the colliery horse keeper and grandson of 'Peg Leg', all served in the army during the War. Alfred, nicknamed 'Punch' as he was an amateur boxer, was a regular soldier in the Cheshire's for 11 years and had an extremely active career. Before the war he served in Palastine, India and the Sudan where he won a medal. During the War he served in Egypt and Malta and fought in North West Europe, where, in 1945, he witnessed a desperate cavalry charge by the Hitler Youth near Nijmegen. As his regiment was armed with machine guns, Alfred could only stare in disbelief as these young fanatics galloped toward them yelling and brandishing swords. Cecil was stationed in Northern Ireland and Levi served as a medic in the Middle East. Eric, my father-in-law, of Constantine Avenue, Heswall, saw action in such places as the Battle of the Bulge, and John, the youngest, served in India. George, another of Ted's sons "did his bit" in the Heswall fire service. Ken, the second youngest was unfortunately unfit for army service due to him being badly scalded as a child when the bottom fell out of a large tea pot as it was passed over him.

Bill Williams was also called up. Bill grew up to become a horseman at *Claremont Farm* in Spital, for a wage of £1.00 a week at the age of 21. In the 1930s, farm workers were given no holidays, so he joined the Territorial Army so that he could go to camp for two weeks every year. Employers could not refuse leave to members of the Territorial Army. When war was declared Bill was automatically called up because he was a trained reservist.

One morning in 1939 Bill received a letter, as did other members of the local T.A. branch of the Cheshires, to report to Bebington Drill Hall. At 10 o'clock on a Saturday morning, buses arrived to take them to Chester camp and families came to see their loved ones off. The men were lined up on parade in front of the commanding officer when a well-dressed lady ran over to him, hugged and kissed him and said "Look after my boy". When the officer recovered his composure he looked at the lines of young men and said to the lady "Which one is he, Madam?" She said "Him" and pointed to the young officer second in command. Sadly, I believe the officer in question, who came from West Kirby, was killed in action.

Bill was injured in a game of football at the army camp and when he came out of hospital his unit had gone overseas. He was sent on a training course and seconded to the Durham Light Infantry. Bill was eventually promoted to Corporal, then Sergeant. Leaving his wife and two children in their tied cottage in Clatterbridge, he was sent into action in North Africa, then Sicily and Italy.

In Italy Bill fought in the bloody battle for the German-held monastery of Monte Cassino where there were extremely heavy casualties. His tough country upbringing, guts and resourcefulness showed through. Bill led many night patrols and it was said he could smell Germans. During an assault on Monte Cassino when his senior officers were killed alongside him, Bill took command and led from the front. He was promoted to Lieutenant on the battlefield. In one sortie Bill went in with 30 men and came out with only 14. His home village of Ness must be very proud of this miner's grandson who is one of the few British Second World War officers to win a field commission. Bill was later promoted to the rank of Captain. He was decorated but says the ones who should have been awarded medals were the women back home such as his wife Jenny, who had to bring up children on their own, endure years of worrying about loved ones in the forces, get by on rations and live through German air raids.

In the years after the pit closed, gradually many of the old cottages in the shadow of the colliery were demolished. *Jacksons Row* was pulled down. This terrace of cottages was named after the colliery Coal Agent Isaac Jackson who lived in the original end cottage for about 50 years. The very old *New Houses* in old Well Lane, Ness, were also demolished. *New Houses* had been the homes of fishermen and colliers since they were built when Well Lane ran down to Denhall Colliery and the River Dee. How old New Houses were, I don't know, but they are on the 1831 map. In the old days this row of cottages got their water from the nearby *Brook Well* in the *Well Field*. This well was reckoned to give the clearest and sweetest water in the area. When it overflowed occasionally, the water ran into a ditch known as the *Broad Brook* which flowed down to the marsh. It was from here Bill Williams gathered water cress for his mother in the summer months.

The old families of the Neston area have always been proud of their heritage and traditions and there are many tales of the old days and the hard way of life. During the 1960s I often went down to Neston to see some mates of mine, and after 1969 when my sister Geraldine moved to Little Neston, I went there even more frequently. A good selection of pubs within a stone's throw of one another made a visit there more interesting. Usually I had been working on a ship in Liverpool during the day and a few pints in Neston at night often brought me in contact with people and accents as different as chalk from cheese. In those days there were still a few men knocking about who had worked at the colliery and a talk with them was always interesting.

The Neston dialect was going strong in those days and still is in a few families. To me the broad accent of the old miners was similar to the old West Wirral accent spoken around the Heswall area years ago, with a smattering of Lancashire and Midlands, rather similar to the old Buckley accent. Many dialect words were used, a few examples being; "skrike" meaning scream, to "munge" someone is to beat them up, to go "wom" is to go home, a greeting of "worrow" means hello, girls were always referred to as "wenches" and "toard" is towards.

Nestoners were always referred to as being "Yusers" by people from the Heswall area and Nestoners called Heswall people "Yowlers". The words "yuse" and "owd'n", being the equivalent of mate, were and still are frequently used. The greeting of "a'reet me owd'n" is an old West Wirral saying meaning "alright my old mate" and was used from Thingwall to Puddington years ago. But the greeting "worrow yuse" is a saying peculiar to the Neston area. The word "yuse" was taken to the Heswall area when Parkgate fishermen moved there.

Dialect sentences baffled people from outside the area and caused me to smile to myself many times when looking at puzzled 'foreigners' listening to a Nestoner. A Nestoner might step back to allow somebody to enter the pub before them saying, "Yoe go fost meowd'n". If the person was a 'Towny' the Nestoner might just as well have spoken in Spanish.

Alas, most of the old characters have passed away, including the daughter of Ellis 'Peg Leg' Roberts', my wife's great-aunt Emily who died in 1991 after living all her 97 years in number 14 New Street. My father-in-law reckons what she didn't know about the colliery area wasn't worth knowing. Emily is buried in Neston churchyard with her mother, father and brother Dick who was tragically killed at the colliery in 1917.

Many of the miners worked hard and played hard. They enjoyed a few pints after a hard days work as their forefathers had done. The large number of old pubs still open in the Neston area are a reminder of the days of hard drinking miners and seaferers. In more recent years the only casualty was the *White Horse* at Neston Cross, managed in the 1960s by Alan Benson and his wife Pat, nee Briscoe, which is now a betting shop.

The mining and seafaring background which produced a breed of tough people in the Neston area was always evident, and a game of football there was a hard battle. Nestoners are gutsy people renowned for standing up for themselves and it's not often I've seen a Neston lad back down. There is plenty of the old miners' spirit in my wife Jenny who is very hard working and either walks or cycles everywhere, including to her sisters in Rock Ferry.

I suppose it's a good thing that a mine with such poor conditions is closed, but on the other hand there is a sense of sadness at the loss of an old local industry and the break up of close knit communities. Today, all the mines in Lancashire and North Wales are closed, the last being the Point of Ayr Colliery on the Welsh side of the River Dee opposite West Kirby, which shut down on Friday 23 August 1996.

What is left of the old area of Little Neston known to the locals as *The Colliery* is still to be found at the bottom of Marshlands Road. The old miners cottages of New Street and Seven Row are still there as well as the *Harp Inn* and what is left of *Denhall Quay*. Most of the Wirral Colliery workings and slag heaps are now under new housing estates. If you have never seen a slag heap, then drive to the bottom of Marshlands Road, park on the marsh car park and walk a few yards in the Parkgate direction. There you will see what is left of the slag heaps of Wirral's last coal mine, closed down in the days when "to smoke a joint" was to burn the Sunday dinner.

Denhall Quay as it is today.
Until the 1850s ships tied up here to load coal, mainly for shipment to Ireland.

HESWALL SLACK

During the last century Heswall, Oldfield and Gayton were thinly populated by families of farmers and farm labourers spread over a wide area. The type of farming was mixed due to the considerable differences in the quality of land which varied from large areas of common and rocky land to good quality soil. In 1811 there were only 59 houses in Heswall-cum-Oldfield and the families were all engaged in agriculture. The total population was 323, made up of 166 males and 157 females. In Gayton were 16 houses containing 19 families, 14 of which were engaged in agriculture. The population was 115, consisting of 66 males and 55 females. Some of the small farmers and labourers made ends meet by working as masons, wheelwrights, shoemakers, thatchers and beer-house keepers etc.

Years ago the village of Heswall was what is today called the Lower Village, and the busy area we see today around Telegraph Road and Pensby Road was called Heswall-on-the Hill. Locals referred to these areas as the Bottom Village and the Top Village. During the last century Heswall-on-the Hill consisted of several small clusters of cottages built on the large rough area of common land called Heswall Hill.

In the early 1800s Heswall Common joined Oldfield, Barnston and Gayton commons. This large area of common land stretched in width roughly from Irby Road and Whitfield Lane, to Pipers Lane, Delavor Road and Dawstone Road. Its length was from Mere Lane and Oldfield Drive, to Milner Road, Mill Lane and Hillside Road. A lane sometimes called Hoylake Road by the locals, ran through the centre of the common and later became Telegraph Road. A glance at the "A to Z" shows just how big this area of common was.

During the early decades of the last century a number of enclosures Acts for this area were passed by Parliament and in many villages, areas of common land were sold off to various individuals. These areas were enclosed for agriculture and a number of cottages were built. Between 1820 and 1850 another 12 enclosures acts were passed affecting common land all over Cheshire. In Heswall 446 acres were earmarked for enclosure. By 1849, Gayton Common, which covered an area from Boundary Lane to Mill Lane, was completely enclosed and made into about two dozen fields.

The common land was very important to the local people. Since ancient times they had had the right to graze their livestock and gather firewood there. Most of the enclosures of Heswall Common were around the perimeter in the areas of what are today The Mount, Rocky Lane, Dawstone Road and Delavor Road. Several patches of land, here and there, within the common were enclosed. In 1831 the population of Heswall, Oldfield and Gayton was 406 living in 75 houses.

Despite all the enclosures, in 1849 Heswall Hills Common still covered 425 acres and the adjoining Oldfield Common consisted of 42 acres 3 roods and 31 perches. The writing was on the wall for Heswall's vast open spaces and gradually year by year more patches of land were cleared and enclosed and more houses built. There was still a considerable amount of Barnston Common remaining, which later became known as Whitfield Common and still exists today.

Here and there, dotted across Heswall Hills Common, were several small isolated hamlets and clusters of cottages with gardens and enclosed crofts. Three groups of three cottages stood within a half-mile radius in areas where today we find Sandy Lane, Heswall British Legion, and Milner Road. The cottages which stood in what is today Milner Road were, in those days, part of an area called *The Slack* owned by the Price family.

The name *slack* is an old local dialect word meaning low lying or a hollow. This name was possibly given to the area as most houses in Heswall, years ago, were on hilly ground.

Out of the nine cottages in the three nearby areas mentioned, in 1849 eight were either owned or occupied by various branches of the Price family. At this time The Slack consisted of three cottages with gardens and crofts amounting to three acres and one rood, with not even a lane for access. One cottage, garden and enclosure was owned and occupied by Thomas Price. The other cottages, gardens and an enclosure were owned by John Price and rented to John Guthery and Joseph Kemp. The other enclosed croft, measuring just over an acre, was rented by Thomas Price from the Lords of the Manor of Heswall.

The 1851 census of Heswall records six families of Prices in Heswall-on-the-Hill and two in the Bottom Village. All the Prices were farmers or farm labourers with small crofts of their own, except William Price of the Bottom Village who was a shoemaker and shopkeeper. Branches of the Price family had moved to various parts of Liverpool, including Islington. Most were brought back to Heswall when they died and were buried in St. Peters Churchyard.

By 1851 the population of Heswall-cum-Oldfield and Gayton had risen to a total of 657. In Heswall-cum-Oldfield lived 513 people in 85 houses and in Gayton 144 resided in 27 houses. Most people were very poor, and many Heswall residents were recorded as paupers.

The Methodist movement in Wirral had been steadily growing. The St. Helens-born pioneer of the Wesleyan Methodist movement, Miles Martindale, was appointed to preach in Wirral. At Storeton he preached several times until eventually a chapel was built there. He was not impressed by the people he met on his travels through Wirral and wrote; *"Wirral contains upwards of 60 villages, the inhabitants are the most ignorant people I have ever laboured among. They consist of farmers and labourers. Avarice and drunkeness are the two demons that undisturbed maintain their sway over the people"*.

Methodism was helped along its way in Heswall by Mrs. Mary Lythgoe from Cumberland, a land proprieter and widow of a Methodist doctor. She started a Sunday School at a house where she lived with the family of George Birch, a slater and plasterer. This house later became a dairy and smallholding called *The Birches* run by Charles Herbert. Today Birches Close off Downham Road South stands on the site. Mary Lythgoe also helped to form the small Wesleyan society which held meetings in cottages belonging to the Price family down *The Slack*.

During the 1850s John Price sold one of his enclosures of just under an acre, and a road was built called Slack Road from what is now Downham Road to Whitfield Lane. A little lane called *The Cop* led from Slack Road to the cottage of Thomas Price and back to Slack Road in a semi-circle.

At this time money was being collected throughout Wirral to build a chapel in Heswall and many small personal donations were made. Eventually, in 1859 a chapel was built in Slack Road at a cost of £213.6s.6d. It was called Gayton Wesleyan Chapel. Despite its name it was not in Gayton but just inside the Heswall boundary.

The congregation consisted of about 60 worshippers, and the organist was Alice Fisher. The chapel elders were Henry Bower of *Little Gayton Hall Farm*, George Hughes of *Prospect Farm*, William Hughes of Barnston, W. Tomlinson of Heswall and Edward Griffiths of Gayton. The first two baptisms were of William Henry Croft of Heswall and Joseph Harris of Brimstage.

Between the Chapel and Price's cottages, new houses were built called *Sandon Terrace* consisting of one row of seven dwellings and another of five, with a cottage on the end called *Elder Cottage*. All except *Elder Cottage* are still standing. Two of these terraced houses were pubs. The first house in the row of seven was called the *Sandon Arms* and the last in the row of five was the *Ebenezer Arms*. All were built by Robert Lightfoot.

The 1861 census of Heswall only lists family details and no road, cottage or farm names are recorded, so it is impossible to know exactly who lived where, but in 1871 some addresses are recorded and the name *Sandon Terrace* is mentioned for the first time. *Sandon Terrace*, and cottages belonging to the Price family, housed 18 families totalling 79 people including lodgers. The following heads of 18 families are recorded in the 16 dwellings standing in The Slack.

NAME	AGE	OCCUPATION	WHERE BORN
John Williams	41	Labourer	Storeton.
Simon Dixon	41	Blacksmith	Whitehaven.
William Smallwood	41	Beerhouse Keep/Landowner	Neston.
Nancy Barlow	40	Washerwoman	Neston.
Margaret Barlow	40	Washerwoman	Barnston.
Joseph Barlow	80		Heswall.
Mary Kemp	49	Charwoman	Heswall.
Daniel Nelson	40	Agricultural Labourer	Bebington.
John Smith	53	Stonemason	Neston.
Elizabeth Hughes	30		Heswall.
Mary Pownall	38	Washerwoman	Heswall.
William Law	35	Agricultural Labourer	Manchester.
Joseph Smith	30	Mason	Neston.
William Roscoe	60	Taylor/Coal Dealer	Puddington.
William Williams	47	Painter	Parkgate.
John Hughes	49	Beerhouse Keeper/joiner	Neston.
Thomas Price	64	Labourer	Heswall.
Thomas Price	66	Agricultural Labourer	Heswall.

Both beerhouses were run by Neston men who were actually wheelwrights by trade. The *Ebenezer Arms* was also a shop as Mary Hughes, the tenant's wife, is recorded as a grocer. Some of the families were quite large and had grandchildren and nephews etc. living with them. Joseph Smith had two boarders living with his family, Thomas Edge, a labourer aged 32 and Jane Edge a 29 year old dressmaker both born in Heswall.

Some of the heads of families were widows but Margaret Barlow is recorded as being married and 'deserted by her husband'. From washerwoman Mrs. Barlow struggling to make ends meet we go to the other extreme circumstances of the Roscoe family a few doors away. Businessman William Roscoe and family appeared to be living quite well, employing 14 year old Charles Mitchel of Leighton as a servant. Also living at the Roscoe's was their five year old niece Eliza Loughlin born in Liverpool, and school mistress Agness Clay aged 17 of Claughton, who might have taught at the Wesleyan Chapel School. The Roscoe family must have been around a bit as one of their children was born in Canada. The water supply for this community was from a well (now capped), in one of the gardens of Sandon Terrace and from another in Boundary Lane.

The Slack was now a village within Heswall township. Heswall was growing all the time and more houses were being built, paths were being made into lanes and lanes into roads. Two lanes were built linking Slack Road to Telegraph Road. One was a short lane called Totty's Road and the other, a bit longer was Lightfoots Lane. Both were named after local farmers. Totty's Road formed part of the boundary between Heswall and Gayton. Because of this, in later years the name was changed to Boundary Lane. The lane named after Elija Lightfoot of Gayton Farm was changed to Mill Lane.

As in any community, as the years pass people die, others move on and some stay, as the change of family names of people down The Slack shows. Details recorded do not always tally exactly, due to genuine mistakes and perhaps ages being recorded in a different month from the previous census. In 1881 *Sandon Terrace* is not named. The area including *Sandon Terrace* and cottages of the Price Family, is listed as *Heswall Slack* and there are 17 families recorded there. Some houses must have had two families living in them. The following heads of families were then recorded.

NAME	AGE	OCCUPATION	WHERE BORN.
William Law	47	Labourer	Manchester.
Isaac Boumphrey	40	Mason	Heswall
Joseph Smith	29	Labourer	Barnston.
William Ellis	43	Labourer	Barnston
William Edge	37	Labourer	Frankby.
Thomas Rutter	36	Labourer	Heswall.
Elizabeth Rathbone	37	Domestic Servant	Barnston.
Timothy Taylor	30	Mason	Tranmere.
Mary Kemp	58		Heswall.
John Peers	50	Farm Labourer	Lt. Neston,
John Smith	35	Mason	Barnston.
Nancy Barlow	52	Laundress	Neston.
Joseph Smith	40	Stone Mason	Neston.
Henry Shone	32	Labourer	Heswall.
John Williams	49	Shepherd	Storeton.
John Hughes	60	Wheelwright	Liverpool.
Mary Pownall	48	Laundress	Heswall.

Two of the three cottages below were, named after a former tenant of the Price family, Joseph Kemp who may have built them for John Price.

Elder Cottage.
Thomas Price	75	Farmer of One Acre	Heswall.

Kemps Cottages
Daniel Hardy	35	Plasterers Labourer	Barnston.
Mary Price	62	Interest in Money	Irby.

Heswall Hills.
Thomas Price	72	Former Ag. Labourer	Heswall.

Isaac Boumphrey, the stone mason is an ancestor of a friend of mine, Ian Boumphrey, the local historian and author. For some unknown reason Joseph Smith and John Hughes do not record the fact that they are also beerhouse keepers and only list their full-time occupations.

Since 1871 John Williams had changed his job from a labourer and had become a shepherd; he still had six of his nine children living with him. Joseph Smith's wife had died and his boarders had moved out. He was bringing up his three children whilst holding down his job as a stone mason, no easy task.

Widow Nancy Barlow was still a washerwoman and she had also made one of her rooms into a shop. She was probably managing reasonably well as her children were grown up and working and her son Thomas was a trainee teacher.

John Smith, the 35 year old mason on the above list, obviously followed in his fathers footsteps as he was the son of John Smith the stone mason recorded in 1871. It appears he was doing well as in 1881 he employed four men. The 58 year old widow Mary Kemp was not recorded as a charwoman, as she was 10 years earlier, although this may have been omitted. Her nephew William whom she brought up, was still living with her and was now an 18 year old labourer.

Widow, Mary Price came to live in *Kemps Cottages* for a few years and then moved on again. She was in a position to pay her way in life as she had no occupation and is listed as living on 'an interest in money'. Thomas Price aged 72 lived in the cottage up The Cop which was part of The Slack but recorded under Heswall Hills as it was set back in an isolated position.

A railway station was opened in Heswall Lower Village in 1886 which linked the area to Hooton and West Kirby. This enabled workers and business men to live in Heswall and travel to work in other areas. Owing to this reliable form of transport more people came to live in the Heswall area and the village continued to grow.

As would be expected, the list of residents recorded as living in Heswall Slack area had changed yet again by 1891; the heads of families were.

NAME	AGE	OCCUPATION	WHERE BORN.
Joseph Smith	39	General Labourer	Woodchurch.
William Law	53		Manchester.
William Ellis	62	Farm Labourer	Liverpool.
John Buckley	42	Fisherman	Chester.
Elizabeth Gerrard	27		Heswall.
Thomas Rutter	43	Farm Labourer	Heswall.
Mary Williams	49	Laundress	Heswall
Mary Kemp	68		Heswall
Helen Jones	57	Dress Maker	Scotland.
John Smith	38	Stone Cutter	Heswall.
Nancy Barlow	61	Laundress	Neston.
Sandon Arms			
Robert Paterson	42	Beerhouse Keeper	Cumberland.
Henry Shone	43	Bricklayers Labourer	Heswall.
George Smith	37	Stonemason	Barnston.
Ebenezer Arms			
George Hughes	27	Bricklayer	Heswall.
Thomas Price	85	Living On Own Means	Heswall.
Thomas Price	82	Retired Gen. Labourer	Heswall.

There are more discrepancies than usual on the 1891 list, not only in the ages but also the places of birth. As always local accents and deafness add to mixups.

This list records the first fishermen in Heswall-on-the-Hill, John Buckley and his 15 year old son. A number of fishermen were attracted to the area partly by the ready market for fish owing to the rise in Heswall's population.

Joseph Smith had his elderly father-in-law Thomas Robinson from Neston living with him and although Thomas was 77 years old, he was still working as a joiner.

Mr. and Mrs. Ellis still had George Gilder, a farm worker from Gloucestershire lodging with them. Mary Kemp's nephew, William, was not recorded as living with her, but her 17 year old granddaughter, Emelia Beaty from Birkenhead, was.

By this time Henry Shone's step-son John Randles had grown up and was working as a horseman groom. Nancy Barlow was still slaving away as a washerwoman or laundress and at this time she had a grandson, a niece and a boarder living with her. The boarder was John Smith senior, the Neston born stonemason. He was still working at his trade although aged 73.

The two Thomas Prices and their wives had reached a reasonable age by Victorian standards. Thomas Price aged 82 and his 72 year old wife Mary had retired. Thomas Price aged 85, and Elizabeth, his 69 year old Chester born wife, were living on their own means, although she was still registered as an upholsterer.

For the first time the pubs are actually recorded by name, previously they were just listed as *Beer House*. The *Ebenezer Arms* was owned by Ralph Robinson of *Thingwall Farm* and bricklayer George Hughes had taken over the tenancy from his father. There was one bed available for travellers and room for 12 drinkers but no stable.

The *Sandon Arms* was owned by Gatehouse & Sons, brewers of Birkenhead. There were no beds for travellers but room for 25 drinkers and a stable with three stalls.

As can be noted from the lists of this small cross-section of the working class community of Heswall Slack, there were masons and bricklayers. This shows that a lot of building was going on in the area, not only of houses but of stone walls, many of which can still be seen in the older parts of Heswall. George Hughes was actually a stone mason by trade but in 1891 he gave his occupation as a bricklayer, which shows a shift from the building of traditional stone cottages to brick houses.

The Methodist movement in Heswall was still growing and a bigger chapel was needed. In 1891 the Wesleyan Centenary Chapel was built on Telegraph Road at a cost of £1,450, commemorating the death of John Wesley, 200 years earlier. Joseph Fisher, formerly of *Oat Hey Farm*, Pensby was activly involved in the building of the new church. Fishers Lane in Pensby was named after him and in his old age he lived at *Rose Mount*, North Drive, Heswall until he died aged 81. There is a brass monument in the church to the memory of Joseph and his wife who were strong Wesleyan Methodists.

The chapel down The Slack was closed and eventually became, of all things, a slaughterhouse, run by the Reddy family to supply their own butchers shops. Giles Reddy originally came to Wirral from Dewsbury in Gloucestershire. He and his wife Elizabeth, from Tranmere, lived in Liscard before moving to Heswall in 1865. Giles was a butcher and farmer. During the 1870s and '80s he farmed 75 acres at *Church Farm* in Heswall Lower Village. His sons Charles, Arthur and John also became butchers.

During the 1890s a railway line was built through mid-Wirral, linking Birkenhead to Chester. In 1896 Heswall Hills station was opened. This extra station further encouraged people who worked in Liverpool, Birkenhead and Wallasey etc. to live in the rural village of Heswall. The population of Heswall-cum-Oldfield rocketed to 2,167 by 1901 and again to 3,616 in 1911. Even sleepy Gayton's population had risen to 238.

All these people needed feeding and the Reddy family butchery business supplied much of the fresh meat. Charlie Reddy took over *Oaklands Farm* in Downham Road North, Burt Reddy ran a butchers shop near the Lydiate and Arthur had one on Pensby Road, close to its junction with Telegraph Road.

Things were changing down The Slack. Not only was there a busy slaughterhouse but shops were being opened as in other areas of Heswall. Many families had come and gone in *Sandon Terrace*. The *Ebenezer Arms* was now a grocers shop run by Annie Ashley and the tenant of the *Sandon Arms* was Lancelot Fisher. Another grocers shop run by Robert Williams had passed to Edmund Jackson by the 1920s, and John O'Neill opened a greengrocers. At this time the roads and lanes of Heswall were patrolled by five Constables and two Sergeants, under Superintendant Thomas Ennion.

Charlie Reddy left *Oaklands Farm* to concentrate on the family butchery business. Years ago there were no supermarkets, fast food, pub grub, vegetarian diets, freezers or fridges. Local people shopped locally and daily for large families. Apart from well-to-do people such as ship owners, there were also a number of cotton brokers living in Heswall before the Wall Street Crash, employing several servants and gardeners, etc. These well-off people often bought meat 28 pounds at a time to feed them and their staff. Butchers shops in Heswall did a roaring trade with quite a few staff kept busy behind the counter and order boys cycling all over the village with deliveries.

The Slack slaughterhouse had become very busy and Charlie Reddy was on the look-out for a first class slaughterman. A big powerful man over six feet tall known as 'Jack Hopper' was offered the job, and he took it.

Reddy's butchers shop in Pensby Road, Heswall at Christmas 1931.

Jack Hopper, whose real name was John Robertson, was born in 1890 at Copperas Hill, Liverpool, of Scottish parents. In those days livestock was driven from Liverpool docks through the streets to slaughterhouses. One day when Jack was a little lad he jumped on a sheep's back as it was driven along his street. The sheep bolted and threw him off, shattering his hip against a kerb stone. As a result, when Jack grew up, one leg was several inches shorter than the other and he wore a special boot. Due to the way he walked because of his accident, people nicknamed him 'Jack Hopper'.

As a young man, Jack worked at a convalescent home in Hoylake and also slaughtered livestock for butchers in the West Kirby and Hoylake area, including Simisters, Price Roberts and James Ball. He was very good at his job as slaughterman and became well known, resulting in Jim Ball offering him a full time job.

Jim Ball had taken over *Oaklands Farm* in Downham Road from Charlie Reddy and had his own small slaughterhouse in the farmyard. After a while Charlie Reddy offered Jack more money to work for him and he accepted. Jack married Ellen Davies, the daughter of the family he was lodging with in *Kemps Cottage* next door to the *Sandon Arms*.

Being not only a butcher but an experienced farmer Charlie Reddy had an eye for good livestock. He used to buy cattle, sheep and pigs from farms all over the Wirral as well as from

Chester, Greasby and Hooton cattle markets. Livestock from further afield such as Chester was transported to Heswall or to Reddy's other shop in Weaverham by rail or by road in Stephen Peers' cattle wagons. Animals bought from local farms or from Hooton and Greasby markets were often driven down the roads and lanes to Charlie's fields on Chester Road, Gayton and *The Far Ends* off Pipers Lane below *The Dungeons*.

The livestock was looked after by 'Yap Up' Lightfoot of Tower Road South. 'Yap Up' got his nickname from the old Heswall farmers when he first worked as a shepherd with his sheep dog. He used to encourage his dog to bark at the sheep to get them moving, by shouting "yap up, yap up". Over the years his nickname somehow changed to 'Yanna'.

Small numbers of cattle and sheep were regularly required for slaughter. Part of 'Yanna's' job was to drive the livestock from the fields, through Heswall to the 'The Slack', often assisted by young local lads including Wilf, Jack Hopper's son, and my father-in-law, Eric Roberts. Apart from Jack Hopper other men employed at the slaughterhouse were Gordon Reddy, Jim Fearon from Sandon Terrace and Jack Hodgkinson from The Mount.

In those days the slaughtering of animals was done by hand and not with a humane killer. Cattle were killed with a blow between the eyes with a pole-axe. To keep the beast steady while it was pole-axed, a rope was tied round its neck and fed through a metal ring fixed in the wall and pulled tight, drawing its head forward. The slaughterman then struck. To finish the beast off, a pith cane, rather like a teacher's cane, was poked through the hole into the animal's brain.

Pigs were stunned by a blow to the head, then stuck in the throat with a sharp knife and bled. Sheep were put in a cradle with three legs tied together before their throats were slit, the free leg would kick and pump the blood out, which was caught in a bucket. Blood from the animals was used for making black puddings. After being slaughtered, all the cattle and sheep were skinned and the skins sold off. This all seems so cruel to us now, but it was a daily scene in those days and neither young nor old thought anything of it.

On Sunday mornings during the 1930s Jack Hopper used to take his son Wilf for long walks to do 'foreigners', and kill a few pigs or lambs at Swift's butchers in Parkgate or at farms in Storeton or somewhere.

Many local families such as Smith, Scott, Davies, Molten, Fearon, Bennett and Kelly lived in *Sandon Terrace* during the 1920s and 1930s. William Smith's wife Annie, nee Duckers was my maternal grandmother's sister.

By the 1930s, houses had been built along both sides of Slack Road. Opposite *Sandon Terrace* in the newer houses were the familiar family names of Flynn, Williams and Sillitoe. There were Sillitoes in Gayton over 120 years ago where their ancestor Daniel, a cotton porter, moved from Oldham in Lancashire.

A new block of shops was doing well, as was the *Sandon Arms* but Slack Road was down to one pub as the *Ebenezer Arms* had closed down at the turn of the century, the last landlord being Jack Peers. The workshop opened by Woodchurch born blacksmith and engineer Joe Lee, next door to the slaughterhouse, was also doing good business. Joe used to repair, service and sharpen lawn mowers and other mechanical equipment which were in regular use by gardeners at the many big houses in the area.

In 1936 Charlie Reddy of *Belleville*, Telegraph Road, died and two years later so did the Heswall slaughterman Jack Hopper. The year after Jack died, the Second World War broke out resulting in meat and all other foods being rationed. Trade in the slaughterhouse slackened off. By 1943 it had closed down and was converted to Heswall Laundry. The laundry eventually closed and became a council yard and the name of Slack Road was changed to Milner Road.

The Cop was changed to Milner Cop and a Territorial Army Centre was opened there by Colonel in Chief of the Royal Artillery, Selwyn Lloyd, who lived in Hoylake.

Of the three original dwellings standing in The Slack area in 1849 and recorded as belonging to the Price family, only the one in Milner Cop is left standing. I believe it was the home of Harry and Ellen Shakeshaft in the 1920s and in later years the Forshaw family. The other two, known as *Kemps Cottages*, which stood between the shops and the *Sandon Arms* were demolished. They were very old and the floors were a step down from road level, consequently when there was a cloud burst they were flooded out. *Elder Cottage*, between *Sandon Terrace* and the slaughterhouse was also demolished.

Regulars outside the Sandon Arms, c. 1936, left to right standing; Walter Hughes, Harry Peters, F. Lawton, Dan Hughes, Matt Davies, Bill Kelly, John Kelly, Percy Rowlands, Ned Stacey senior, Bert Clayton, Percy Fisher (pub manager holding up two bottles of beer), Dan Sillitoe, Arthur Wilson, G. Williams, Alf Fleming and Tom Adams. Left to right sitting. Mr. Hughes, Sammy Buckley (smoking pipe, was a fisherman's son born Sandon Terrace 1885), Ben Francom, P. Bufton, George Campbell, Brian Smith (boy), Ted Davies, Ned Stacey junior and Ted Roberts (ex Neston coalminer): The above Ben Francom was an exceptionally good runner and took after his father who competed in the Olympics. During the war Ben was captured and re-captured several times. To prevent him from running away, the Germans shot him in the foot.

There were some right characters in Heswall in those days. Annie Ashley of the grocers shop, formerly the *Ebenezer Arms*, sold, among other things, twist tobbacco at so much per inch and she had a brass rule fixed on the counter for measuring various goods. Out of the blue she took bad and was confined to her bed for a while. Her sister, who knew nothing about the shop was asked to fill in for her. One of the local comedians came in and asked for so many penn'orth of 'bacca'. Annie's sister asked the man how it was sold. He said "by the yard", she fell for it, and he made off with a couple of months supply of twist.

One well known joker was Rob Tarbuck. He married Ada Reddy in 1912 and they ran a fishmongers and poulterers shop in Pensby Road, Heswall. Rob was a fanatical supporter of Heswall football team, as many locals were in those days, but the opportunities for seeing the professional game were very limited. Upwards of 500 supporters sometimes turned up for Heswall's important matches, particularly those against Neston.

One Saturday afternoon Heswall were to play in a cup match on their pitch, which in those days was where Border Road is now. Unfortunately for some regular supporters, the game fell on the same day as an important bowls match on the *Sandon Arms* green, now the pub car park. Rob came to the rescue and let it be known that he would take his 12 bore shotgun to the match and when Heswall scored he would fire a barrel into the air. Word of the plan spread all over Heswall and those who could not get to the game for one reason or another were all ears.

On the afternoon of the match Rob Tarbuck walked the touch line wearing a top hat and claw hammer coat, with his 12 bore under his arm. Lucky enough Heswall scored several times and each time he fired his shot gun, a cheer went up all over Heswall. There was no traffic in those days and the blast was heard for miles.

Another character was Siddy Prince who often took gate receipts at Heswall football matches and was bit of a hard case when necessary. When one particular match was due to start, a gang of Neston lads turned up to watch. As they approached the gate Siddy said, "that'll be thruppence apiece lads". The leader of the gang tried to push past saying "you'll get no thruppence off me yuse". Siddy stepped back and punched the Nestoner between the eyes and he went down like a sack of spuds. As the rest of the gang stared at their hero on lying on the grass Siddy held up his fist and asked "does anybody else want a dose of this medicine while the cork's out of the bottle". The rest of the gang paid up.

The Sandon Arms and Sandon Terrace, September 1996.

I used to walk down Milner Road regularly in the 1960s for a few pints of Threlfall's ale in the *Sandon Arms* or *The Slack*, as the pub has always been nicknamed. In those days it was a typical old pub with a long narrow bar, lounge, snooker room and a music room with a piano.

It was a popular pub with people of all ages and there was always a good atmosphere. In 1970 I came home from sea to find the place had been modernised and the four rooms had been knocked into two. Since then it has been made into one big room.

Heswall has gradually grown into a town. When I was a lad all the locals more or less knew one another, at least by sight. When we went to a dance down The Mount or in a church hall or somewhere and the lights came on in the interval, everyone looked round at all the familiar faces. If a stranger was there, you would hear people say, "who's that?". These days when I go out and look around me, it is more like 'spot the local'.

The *Sandon Arms*, like the old Slack Road, has changed over the years, just as everywhere else has. But to me the old cottages of *Sandon Terrace* still look nice with plenty of character and remind me of old Heswall. Today it is hard to believe that these two rows of Victorian terraced houses were once surrounded by hundreds of acres of farmland and common. A little isolated country community, with small farms, shops, pubs, a chapel and a school.

Today there are descendants of nearly all the families mentioned still living locally, although branches of some of them, including Reddys, Tottys and Prices emigrated to Australia and New Zealand.

Jack 'Hopper' Robertson had three sons, Stewart, Ken and Wilf. I knew Stewart quite well, he lived on his smallholding called *Watsonia* on the Chester High Road and kept geese, pigs and sheep as well as working as a driver. He was a really nice bloke, but unfortunately he died of cancer in 1987. Ken lives in Surrey and Wilf lives in Irby. I know Wilf Robertson well, he is retired now but can often be found helping out in reception at the Irby Club. Wilf has led a very active and interesting life, having seen action whilst serving our country in the Second World War, first in the Royal Artillery and then the Parachute Regiment. After the war he worked as a postman in Heswall for 11 years and then in the ambulance service for 24 years until his well-earned retirement.

There are numerous members of the Price family around the Heswall area. The property of Thomas Price senior of Sandy Lane (in those days called Heather Road) has stayed in the family, eventually passing to Miss Annie Price. This property included two of the three old farm cottages recorded on the tithe map of 1849, called *Rose Cottage* and *Plum Tree Cottage*. The other cottage which once stood at the bottom of Price's private lane, was sold and eventually became the home of the Griffiths family. It was knocked down when Hesselwell Court, (next to the *Harvest Mouse* pub) was built.

The Price family were evidently very religious in the last century and not only were their cottages down The Slack used for prayer meetings but so was *Plum Tree Cottage*. Eventually the Presbyterian congregation in Sandy Lane became too big for the old cottage, and a Tabernacle, then a church was erected opposite the Puddydale, now replaced by the modern United Reformed Church next to Tesco's.

When Annie Price passed away she left to her sister's son, Walter Price Smith several old cottages including *Plum Tree Cottage* and *Rose Cottage* which was once a beerhouse called the *Lord Nelson*. Walter was born in the old cottages in Sandy Lane in 1919. He was named after his uncle Walter who was killed in the Great War.

Walter himself served right through the Second World War. Whilst training in Scotland he met his wife Margaret, a farmer's daughter from Lanark. After they married Walter and Margaret settled in their smallholding in Sandy Lane, Heswall. Margaret brought her own pigs down from Scotland to help stock up.

Walter was a very friendly man who had a tremendous knowledge of the Heswall area. In his younger days he used to go shooting on many of the local farms and seemed to know everyone.

Sadly Walter Price Smith died in January 1994 and Heswall lost a very pleasant character. A service was held for him in the old chapel at *Plum Tree Cottage*, the small seven acre farm which has been in his family for over 150 years. He is sadly missed by his wife Margaret and family, people in the Sandy Lane area and all who knew him.

Walter's cousin, Alan Smith a retired landscape gardener and lawnmower engineer of Whaley Lane, Irby has taken a lifelong interest in Heswall and in particular the Sandy Lane area where he was born and bred. As Alan says, "Gone are the days when Jack Hopper would wander down Sandy Lane on a Sunday morning to kill a pig for his grandfather old 'Slasher' Smith and go halves with it after he had hung and cured it". But the old sandstone cottages along Sandy Lane, including what was Maysies shop, *Builth Cottages, Heather Cottage, Rose Cottage* and *Plum Tree Cottage*, which were home to such local families as Fell, Nicholls, Calveley, Apter, Gardener, Lindfield, Jones, Smith, Wilbraham and Price, are all still standing. These old cottages have great character and together with *Sandon Terrace* are some of the few surviving dwellings of yesteryear's Heswall-on-the-Hill.

Below are some Heswall road names which have changed from 100 years ago when some of the longer ones were made up from two shorter lanes.

ROAD NAME IN 1890s.	ROAD NAME IN 1990s.
Slack Road	Milner Road
Heather Road	Sandy Lane
Totty's Road	Boundary Lane
Lightfoot's Lane	Mill Lane
Railway Road	Davenport Road
Dixons Road	Rocky Lane (lower end)
Hillhouse Road	Rocky Lane (upper end)
Pinnacle Road	Beacon Lane
Liverpool Road	The Mount
Bungalow Hill	Thurstaston Road (lower end)
Gents Road	Thurstaston Road (upper end)
Back Lane	West Grove
Colledge Road	Hillside Road
Hillside Road	Dawstone Road (Wallrake to Well Lane)
Dawstone Lane	Dawstone Road (Rocky Lane to Wallrake)
Gilberts Lane	Delavor Road (from Farr Hall Rd. up)
Scabbrook Hill	Delavor Road (from Farr Hall Rd. down)

Below is a list of pubs in Heswall, Gayton and Barnston in Victorian days.

NAME OF PUB	LOCATION
HESWALL.	
Black Horse	School Hill
Lord Nelson	Sandy Lane
Dee View	Dee View Road
Ebenezer Arms	Milner Road
Sandon Arms	Milner Road
Ship Inn	Village Road
White Lion	Wallrake
Hotel Victoria	Gayton Road
GAYTON.	
Glegg Arms	Chester Road
Old Three Pigeons	Mill Lane
BARNSTON.	
Fox and Hounds	Barnston Village
Spencers Beerhouse	Barnston Village

Some of these pubs have had their names changed several times. The *Black Horse* changed to the *Heswall Hotel* then back to the *Black Horse*. The *Fox and Hounds* was originally called the *Black Horse*, then the *Fox and Hounds*, during the 1890s it was called the *Sportsman Arms* for a while, then changed back to the *Fox and Hounds*.

The *Dee View* was changed to the *Letters* then back to the *Dee View*. The Ellis family ran the *Dee View* from the 1870s to the turn of the century. Emmanuel 'One Pint' Ellis was a bit of a character. For some reason or other he would only serve a man on his way home from work one pint. After the man had finished his ale he would would say "get off home to your wife (or mother) and have your tea, then if you want to come back I'll serve you all you want". What the reason behind this was I don't know. Maybe a friend or relation used to go drinking straight from work and ruined his home life and Emmanuel decided he did not want to be responsible for anyone else's downfall. There are one or two women about today who wish all landlords were 'One Pint' Ellis.

Old sandstone cottages of different ages, shapes and sizes built by the Price family in Sandy Lane.

HILBRE ISLANDS

Hilbre Islands were almost certainly part of the Wirral mainland in prehistoric times. It has been suggested that originally they would have been one large island. There was believed to be a Bronze age settlement on the island which would have given reasonable security, as no-one could approach without being seen. In those days there would possibly have been enough farm land to help support an extended family group or clan, with the added advantage of plenty of fish and shellfish.

Metal objects, pottery and glass from the Roman period have been found on the island. The Romans were believed to have had an observation post there to keep an eye on shipping going to and from Chester. After the Romans left Wirral in about 410 the local Celts probably made use of the Island until 615, when Wirral was conquered by the Angles under the leadership of Aethelfrith.

A cell of Anglo-Saxon Benedictine monks settled on the Island and a burial ground has been found. This small island became known as St. Hildeburgh's Eye, possibly after being dedicated to the 7th century Saint, St. Edburge of Mercia. The Vikings who frequently sailed the River Dee would have been familiar with the island, where the treacherous rocks to the south are still called *Tanskey Rocks*. The name *Tanskey* probably comes from the Norse words *tonn* a tooth, *sker* a reef and *eye* a small island, meaning the island with rocks like teeth.

After 1066 the two Anglo-Saxon monks were replaced by two Norman monks. William the Conqueror's nephew, Earl Hugh of Averanches, gave a number of Wirral Manors to Robert de Rodelant, Baron of Rhuddlan, who was his cousin and Commander-in-Chief. The manors given to Robert were Great and Little Mollington, Leighton, Thornton, Gayton, Heswall, Thurstaston, Wallasey, Great and Little Meols, and Caldy including the village of West Kirby. Hilbre Island was part of the manor of Caldy.

The Bishops Transcripts include the following description:
WEST KIRBY. This village and the advouson of the Church were given by Robert (Richard writes the ledger book) together with the Church of the Island adjoining viz. Hildeburshay [now Hilbre] & the Church of St. Peter in Chester to the Abbey of Utica in Normandy wherein his ancestors were buried, and not long after the Abbot & Convent of St. Ebrulfe released, or rather sold those places to the Abbot and Convent of Chester for 30 shillings a year to be paid at their manor of Totheling at the charges of the Monks of Cheshire.

Reference is made in this very old document to the *Church of the Island* which was believed to have been a chapel dedicated to the Virgin Mary. The island and chapel became a detached part of St. Oswalds parish in Chester, owned by St. Werburgh's Abbey.

In 1088 Robert of Rhuddlan was killed at Deganwy by the Welsh. Some of his lands eventually passed down to Robert Lancelyn who, in about 1190 granted the monks £3 a year from the manor of Little Meols. A tenement in Meols, as well as the fishery and lake (later called Hoyle Lake) was given to the monks by Robert Lancelyn's son William.

During the 1300s the island became a place of pilgrimage to Our Lady of Hilbre and the offerings helped maintain the cell of monks who lived there undisturbed until the Dissolution. The monks probably also maintained a beacon fire as a guide to Chester bound ships.

Henry VIII had for a considerable time sought to divorce his brother's widow, Catherine of Aragon and marry Anne Boleyn, with the Pope's blessing. Negotiations dragged on for years. Tired of waiting, Henry declared the Act of Supremacy, replacing the Pope with himself as Supreme Head of the English Church. He divorced Catherine, and in 1539 a copy of the Bible, translated from Latin into English, was placed in every church. In the same year the

Dissolution of the Monasteries was ordered and the cell on Hilbre Island, along with every monastery in the land was closed. Henry VIII believed he was a true Catholic to the end of his days.

One of the monks, Robert Harden, left the island to become a priest at West Kirby, whilst the other monk, Robert Wigan, stayed on the island and made a living from farming and fishing.

Hilbre in those days was a very important little port, and there is ample evidence of this. During the 1500s a lot of shipping was registered as being "of Hilbre". Below is a list (4) of Wirral shipping (as originally spelt) for the 35 days from 27 October to 30 December 1544, all of which paid dues to Chester as they were Chester 'creek' ports.

DATE	NAME OF SHIP	HOME PORT	NAME OF MASTER
XXVII Oct.	The Nottorke	Helbre	Richard Lytill
XXX Oct.	The Michaelle	Hilbre	Thomas Lytill
II Nov.	?	Hilbre	Rob. Radcliff [of Greasby]
III Nov.	The Marten	Neston	Richard Kempe
X Nov.	The Peter	Hilbre	Richard Sheppard
XII Nov.	The Trinitie	West Kerkbye	Peter Warrington
XIII Nov.	The Rose ?	West Kirkbye	Thomas Wright
XIII Nov.	The Christopher	Hilbre	John Wright
XXII Nov.	The Marten	Neston	Richard Kempe
XXIV Nov.	The Pride	West Kirkbye	John Couentrye
? Dec.	The Goodlocke	Code [Caldy]	Thomas Hogg
XXIV Dec.	The Nuttock	Hilbre	Richard Lytill

This shows how busy Hilbre was compared with other nearby Wirral ports. The popularity of the island port was probably due to it being a good anchorage, close to the open sea, therefore mariners did not have to navigate channels as they would to reach other ports. The sandbanks protected the Hilbre anchorages by breaking the force of the waves. As would be expected at a small port in 1544, the vessels listed above were small, being between five and sixteen tons. They were usually taken to sea by their owners who were often farmers or fishermen from neighbouring villages. The cargoes were mainly herrings, sheep skins, wool, coal and corn, which may have been taken to and from Hilbre by other small boats. Some goods would have been carted or taken by pack horse across the sands, to and from West Kirby, Caldy and Dawpool.

During the later 1500s there were more boats recorded as being of Hilbre than of all the other Wirral ports put together. After Chester and Liverpool, Hilbre was the most important port in the Dee / Mersey area. In 1571 there were 10 ships using Hilbre as the home port and one using West Kirby. The following year there were also several ships sailing from Heswall.

Most of the trade was with Ireland. Cargoes of coal from the Deeside pits, sugar, cloth, knives etc. were shipped mainly to Dublin. The boats returned to the Dee full of animal skins for the Chester leather industry. Most skins were from sheep or lambs but many were from various Irish wild animals including martens, otters, foxes and wolves.

Not all the trade and activity was honest. In 1585 a ship was stolen from a Wirral port by pirates who could not navigate it through the channel and were caught on Hilbre.

There was a customs house and beer house on the island. The beer house was probably a rough dive frequented by some unusual characters, from rough and ready honest mariners, shipowners and soldiers to smugglers and wreckers. Trade would be very good at times when men waiting for bad weather to clear probably did a lot of heavy drinking.

The following quote (5) illustrates just how busy and important Hilbre was in this period of our history for transporting troops mustered at Chester, across the sea to Ireland:

The army, consisting in list of 4000 foote and 200 horse, whereof 3000 of the foote and all the horse were levied in England, the other 1000 foote were taken of the old companys about Dublin, and and all assigned to meette att Knockfergus [Carrickfergus] the first of May; that part levyed in England was shipt at Helbree, neere unto West-Chester, on the 24th of April, 1600. And of these a regiament of a 1000 foote and 50 horse were to be taken out imediatelie upon our landing, and assigned to Sr. Mathew Morgan to make a plantation with, att Ballishannon.

Soldiers on route to Ireland sometimes waited at Hilbre for favourable winds for their ship. One ship used for troop movements in 1600 was the *Angel of Hilbre*. Soldiers and horses were also shipped at Neston, Hoylake, Liverpool and other local ports. The fleet then gathered off Hilbre before setting sail for Ireland.

There were probably a few people living on the islands during the 1600s and a number of buildings for travellers to stay in whilst waiting for a change in the weather. Brownbill writes of a survey in 1737 recording the ruins of houses and a mill on Middle Island.

Obviously the inn keeper and his family lived on Hilbre and possibly others. A marriage recorded in 1762 is of Thomas Parr of West Kirby parish to Mary Rimmer of Hilbre Island in the parish of St. Oswald, Chester. There were also deaths recorded; on 29 January 1764, William Pritchard, a passenger on a sloop at Hilbre, was found washed up on the island.

During the early 1800s, Hilbre was said to be the venue for bare knuckle and cock fights. When the tide was in, gamblers and participants were safe from interference from the law. The old pub on the island probably did a roaring trade. It was believed to have been called the *Seagull Inn* and closed in the late 1820s.

Bodies were regularly found on or near Hilbre in this period. Margaret Corfe aged 92 was found dead on Hilbre Island in May 1821. Whether she was a resident of the island or a visitor out for a stroll which proved too much for her, I don't know. In those days large numbers of people from Welsh villages crossed the Dee on foot to get to Neston Market, wading the channel at low tide. Every now and again somebody was drowned, particularly if fog or mist came rolling in causing travellers to lose their bearings.

In 1825 the bodies of a husband and wife named Phillips from Holywell were found two days apart, the husband near Hilbre and the wife on Caldy shore. Between 1826 and 1835 the bodies of at least seven people were found washed up around Hilbre.

The 1841 census records a number of workmen, two families and two farm servants living on the island, a total of 19 people. They were Stephen Barnett, aged 35 born in Margate, Kent, who was registered as a mariner and attendant on the buoy, his 35 year old wife Mary Anne, born in Sandwich, their three children and Mary Hewitt, a 15 year old farm servant. In another cottage lived Thomas Matthews, the telegraph keeper, his wife Elizabeth, their three children and Elizabeth Evans a 20 year old farm servant. The telegraph was used to relay the movement of ships to Liverpool and Holyhead.

At this time the telegraph station and lookout station were being built. There were five stonemasons and two labourers living and working there. The stonemasons were John Parry, Joseph and William Captree, Edward Taylor and William Firfield. The two labourers were Irishman Edward Mulroony and 25 year old James Hignett; James was the only adult on the island born in Cheshire.

Buildings on the island included a barn, a goathouse and a pigsty. I don't know for certain what animals the two young girls registered as farm servants would have looked after, but they probably included a pony for transport, either a milking cow or goats (possibly both) sheep, poultry, pigs and rabbits. The two large islands, Hilbre (11 acres) and Middle Island (5 acres) were divided into crofts for growing hay and corn and grazing livestock. There were also kitchen gardens where vegetables grew well in the rich peaty soil. Fresh water came from a well about 40 feet deep which the monks were believed to have sunk through the solid rock.

The Hilbre people would have been as self sufficient as possible, as shops and markets were far away and tides and bad weather made regular timetable journeys impossible. The small island, then called Little Lee, now Little Eye was only a glorified rock and no use for anything. It is now being left to erode away to nothing, and will probably be gone within a few years.

There was something of a population explosion on the Island in the 1840s, with Lucy Barnett born there in 1840, William Henry Matthews in 1841 and Elizabeth Matthews in 1842. Sadly there was a burial also in 1842, it was that of Thomas Matthews the 47 year old telegraph keeper and father of the two babies.

Bagshaws Directory of 1850 quotes the following:
Hilbree Island, an extra parochial liberty, forms part of St. Oswald parish, Chester, and is about 20 miles N.N.E. from that city. A cell of monks were established here, which was dedicated to the Virgin Mary. Hollinshead says, "thither went a set of superstitious fools on pilgrimage to our Lady of Hilbery, by whos offerings the monks there were cherished and maintained". Bradshaw in his marvellous life of St. Werburgh, gives an account of the miraculous interference of that Saint on behalf of the Earl of Chester. He was on a pilgrimage to the well of St. Winefred opposite, when he was attacked by a strong party of Welsh, and forced to take shelter in Basingwerk Abbey. The insecurity, however, of this place, induced him to appeal to St. Werburgh, and the saint instantly threw up sand banks, which separated the waters, and the Baron of Halton, his constable, came to his succour with a body of troops, and rescued him from his peril. The wonderful intervention of the saint gave great celebrity to the island, and the pious monks profited no little by the credulity of the visitors. There is not the slightest relic of this religious establishment left. Land marks are fixed on the island for the purpose of assisting the navigation into Hoyle Lake. There are two houses on the island, the residents are employed in inspecting the buoys and telegraph. The island contains about ten statute acres.

A lifeboat station and accomodation for lifeboatmen was built on the island in 1850 but the crew was based at Hoylake.

The census of 1851 records only 10 people living in the two island cottages and no building workers. The Trinity House buoy attendant, Stephen Barnett and family still lived in *Family Cottage*, but there was no record of the two farm servants.

In *Telegraph Cottage* lived a new telegraph keeper with his wife, three children and an assistant keeper. He was Liverpool born Thomas Hughes, a 46 year old ex-mariner whose 35 year old wife Phinea was born in Wakefield. The assistant telegraph keeper was 19 year old Joseph Roberts from West Kirby.

Professor Craggs records that Thomas Hughes' first wife was tragically lost shortly after they went to live on the island in the early 1840s. She had been to market to buy a few sheep for the island farm. Whilst crossing the sands from West Kirby with the sheep in her pony and trap, she lost her way in a snow storm and was drowned.

In 1853 a red sandstone cross was found on Hilbre, possibly of Irish design made in the 9th or 10th century. The Church sold Hilbre to the Mersey Docks and Harbour Board in 1856.

During the 1860s the Barnett's and the Hughes' were still employed on the Island and the population had fallen to seven. Patrick Dealy a 27 year old general servant lived with the

Barnetts, and probably looked after the farm animals and kitchen garden. It appears the Barnett children had all grown up and flown the nest. Lucy Barnett who was born there 21 years before, married George Lees of Birmingham in 1861. Thomas Hughes still had two daughters living at home and one of them, worked as his telegraph assistant until he died in 1870.

By 1871 there was quite a change of personnel on the island, with newcomers from Wales. Thomas Hughes' widow Phinea, and two of her daughters were still there. Phinea was registered as 'out of business', but daughter Isabella was down as assistant telegraph keeper to telegraph manager, Morris Griffiths. Morris was born in Llanddonlas in Denbighshire and his wife Eleanor was from Rhuddlan.

Hilbre Islands from Red Rocks.

The Barnetts had left, and the new Trinity buoy-keeper and occupier of *Family Cottage* was Thomas Owens. Thomas had come to Hilbre from Haverford-West in South Wales with his wife Tasnie, son Thomas and 14 year old nephew who was registered as an assistant buoy painter. Thomas and his wife also had a two month old baby, probably born on the island, which then had 10 inhabitants. They had had bad luck two years earlier when their six month old baby son William died.

By the late 1870s the job of Trinity House buoy-keeper had ceased and the cottage was then leased to several private individuals, one of which was Henry Daubeney Brandreth, an American-born merchant of Little Meols.

In the telegraph station things were much the same. The census of 1881 records Morris Griffiths still telegraph and tide gauge keeper, and Isabella Hughes as his assistant. Her sister had left, and only four people now lived on the island.

The census of 1891 records that the job of Telegraphist had passed to another married Welshman, 32 year old Lewis Jones. Lewis and his 34 year old wife Ellen were both Anglesey born, in the villages of Llaneilian and Llanrbyalial respectively. (Llaneilian is east of Amlwch but the second place name does not exist and must have been mis-spelt. It could possibly be Llanrhuddlad near Church Bay).

Part of *Family Cottage*, the former home of the Trinity House buoy keepers, had been made into a clubhouse for the Mersey Canoe Club. The caretaker was 28 year old Louisa Anderson, born in Rock Ferry, who had four young children, Florence eight, Richard six, Louisa three and Harold aged one. Also living in *Family Cottage* were John Vernon a 22 year old farm servant, and domestic servant Sarah Brant aged 13, both born in Liverpool. Staying in the Hilbre Island Canoe Club for one reason or another were two club members and a visitor. The two club members were William Wynne, a bank accountant born in Uttoxeter and Townson Rundell, an average adjuster, born in Falmouth, both aged 38. The visitor was 34 year old John Jellicoe, an insurance agent from Limerick, Ireland.

In 1896 the Hilbre Yacht Club was formed and based at the island using their yacht, the *Hilbre*.

With the coming of the railway to West Kirby day trippers crossed the sands in great numbers and packed Hilbre Islands causing so much concern that visiting permits were issued. On bank holidays policemen were needed to monitor the crowds and check permits. Three bungalows for yacht owners were built and in 1911 iron railings were fixed around the two larger islands. Those without permits caught out by the tide, had to climb the cliffs and hang on to the railings until the tide ebbed.

During the Great War Birkenhead was a defended port protected by a special reserve battalion of the Cheshire Regiment. The 16 officers and 500 men of the battalion were under the command of Lieut. Colonel Logan D.S.O. who deployed them to defend Birkenhead docks and positions of strategic importance across Wirral. These strategic positions included Hilbre Islands which had a garrison of 21 men. Unfortunately Colonel Logan was killed at Loos in France while in charge of the 15th Durham Light Infantry.

Lewis Jones the Telegraph Keeper retired in 1923 after well over 30 years on the island and was succeeded by Mr. Thomas who was the last Keeper. In 1939 the Telegraph Station was closed down and the R.A.F. set up a machine gun post there. During the Second World War, the R.A.F. used Hilbre as part of a decoy system, set up to confuse German bombers targeting Liverpool. After the war the islands were sold to Hoylake U.D.C. who appointed a resident custodian.

Nowadays fishermen and bird watchers enjoy themselves in an ideal location for their chosen pastimes. Many rare birds have been seen there as well as local ones which you would not expect to visit the islands, such as owls, kingfishers and partridge. About eight common species often nest there, including the wren and the dunnock. In 1962 Hoylake Council built a bird watching hut. Birds are sometimes caught and ringed to monitor their movements. Over the years many different animals have also been recorded on the islands, including the fox, otter, stoat, rabbit, hedgehog and bats. The seals seen on the sandbanks appear to be increasing in numbers, yet fish stocks are getting lower.

In 1974 the Metropolitan Borough of Wirral took over the islands. Although archaeologists have gone over the islands with a fine-tooth comb there are still small finds being made. One such find was made on a wet March day in 1989 by Rolph Jordan of Irby (the lad who drew the sketches in the mining chapter). It was Rolph's first visit to Hilbre. On the far side of the main island, in a cleft in the rocks on the shore, he found an old copper penny. On one side was a harp and the date 1816, with the Duke of Wellington on the other side. As the Duke had been facing upwards he had been worn by the tide. Rolph did some quick research and found that unfortunately the coin was a worthless Irish token. But nevertheless it goes to show that if you get out and about there are still things to be found.

Today Hilbre Islands are still as pleasant a day out as ever, particularly when not too busy. The 1½ mile stroll out there, a lap of the islands, a look in the caves and a potter round the rock pools is a nice break, but time and tide have to be watched. Many people have been caught on sandbanks by the tide which rushes down gutters and can rise at a rate of two inches per minute. Mist and fog have also caused people to lose their way and be cut off. There have been many nasty falls on the rocks including one in the 1960s when a man died after falling into the sea. We will never know how many lives have been lost going to and from Hilbre over the centuries, but I bet it is no small number.

It is quite safe to cross to and from the islands as long as the tide is not on the turn and there is no mist, but before setting off people should read the notice board at Dee Lane and on no account cross to the islands from Red Rocks.

An aerial view of Hilbre Islands. The old lifeboat slipway can clearly be seen.

LITTLE MEOLS

Little Meols was an ancient village on the north-west corner of Wirral, which today, along with the forgotten village of Hoose, forms Hoylake. (The name Hoose is preserved as the electoral ward and the name of a mundane block of flats, but is otherwise obsolete).

The boundary of Little Meols ran from Red Rocks, down the Dee coast to West Kirby, inland along the line of Bridge Road and the River Birket, then turned again to follow the line of Lake Place to the sea, and finally back along the shore to Red Rocks.

Before and during the Roman occupation of Britain, a Celtic settlement was situated not far away at Dove Point, Great Meols. The many different coins, brooches and other objects found on the beach at Meols, and recorded by Hume in 1863, prove that the settlement was a thriving port, trading mainly with other English ports as well as Wales and Ireland.

After defeating the Celtic Britons at Chester in about 615 Anglo-Saxons began to settle in Wirral. In later years Vikings also settled the area followed by the Normans. After invading England in 1066 the Normans eventually subdued Wirral along with the rest of Cheshire in 1070.

The Domesday book written in 1086 records that Little Meols was previously held by the Anglo-Saxon Leofnoth, who also held Great Meols and the coastal villages of Caldy, Thurstaston, Gayton and Leighton. After the conquest, Little Meols and many other Wirral villages were granted to Robert de Rodelant, Baron of Rhuddlan.

In the Domesday book the following is written of Little Meols; *Leofnoth held it, one hide paying tax, land for 1½ ploughs. One rider, two villagers, and two smallholders have one plough. Value before 1066, 15 shillings (75p), now 10 shillings (50p), found waste.*

Great Meols had one hide paying tax, land for three ploughs and the inhabitants recorded were one rider, three villagers and three smallholders. Hoose did not exist as a village in this period and is not mentioned until the later 1100s.

A hide was about 120 acres, a rider or riding man kept an eye on roads, bridges and the manor in general, assisting the Lord when and where necessary. The population of the village might have been about 30 if each man recorded had a wife and four children, which was probable in those days. Found waste, probably meant that Little Meols was one of the villages burned in retaliation for Cheshire resisting William the Conqueror's rule.

After Robert of Rhuddlan's death the village of Little Meols eventually passed to the Monks of St. Werburgh and over the centuries to the Lancelyn family and the Meolse family.

The subsidy rolls drawn up in 1545 record seven people in Little Meols and nine in Great Meols as paying tax. Very poor people would not have to pay any. The tax payers recorded were heads of families, therefore the population of Little Meols, rich and poor, could have been between 60 or 70. The tax payers in Little Meols (in Latin) were Johe Lyttle, Johe Browne, Elena Browne, Edwardo Wryght, Thoma Wryght, Ricardo Shurleacre and Johe Rimmer. All these old Wirral family names still survive; Shurleacre became Sherlock.

The Hoyle Lake or High Lake (as it was also known, owing to its depth) was the reason for the area's shipping and relative prosperity. The lake was a natural anchorage, half a mile wide and between 15 and 30 feet deep at low tide, protected by high sandbanks. The small cluster of houses close to the lake became known as Hoylake. Seafarers and fishermen did not refer to the villages as Hoose or Little Meols. As far as they were concerned they were anchored at Hoyle Lake and that is what they called the area. There are numerous mentions of the old anchorage of Hoylake during the 1600 and 1700s. The first written record of the modern spelling of Hoylake, was in 1689 when the Royal Yacht *Monmouth* sailed through Hoylake after being serviced at Parkgate.

The most famous sailing from Hoyle Lake was that of the army of William of Orange on its way to Ireland to fight the forces of the former king, James II, as is recorded by Rev. George Storey, chaplain to the regiment: *In June 1689 most of them were commanded to Chester, in order to be shipped for Ireland. Most of them encamp about a week at Neston, and then on Thursday the 8th August, about six o'clock in the morning, His Grace, Duke Scomberg, General of all their Majesties Forces, Count Solmes, General of the Foot, and several great officers more, with ... 10,000 foot and horse, embarked at Highlake for Ireland.*

The troop ships lay at Hoyle Lake waiting for favourable winds. On Monday the 12th at four o'clock in the morning the wind blew S.S.E. and S.E. The frigate *Bonaventure* fired a gun and lit the main top mast shrouds, which was the signal to prepare for sailing. By six o'clock the fleet of about 90 vessels was under sail, and at eight o'clock all the Captains and Masters received orders to sail for Carrickfergus Bay in Ireland.

The Kings Gap, an old highway leading to the sea.

Regular reinforcements were sent from Hoylake to Ireland, Dean Davies records in April 1690: *We dined at our lodgings in Chester and after dinner they all grew very busy in sending their things away to Hoylake, where lay our recruits of horse, being 400 and the Nassau and Brandenberg regiments.*

Two months later William III, Prince of Orange was on his way to Hoyle Lake to take ship for Ireland. His men encamped on the plain between Great Meols and Wallasey, known as the Leasowes. On 12 June, William of Orange and the Prince of Denmark set sail for Carrickfergus. The lane in Little Meols which they travelled along to the Hoyle Lake still bears the name "The Kings Gap". After arriving in Ireland, William led his united army consisting of troops from nearly every Protestant nation to victory over the Jacobite forces of James II and his French allies at the Battle of the Boyne.

These large numbers of troops probably lost quite a few personal items while camped on the Leasowes; Hume records that 42 coins from the reign of William of Orange had been found in the area. This figure must have been a fraction of what had been lost as it was only what he personally knew about in the days before metal detectors.

Other mentions of the anchorage include that, in 1756, impressed men held aboard a tender called the *Bolton,* at Hoylake, mutinying and taking over the vessel after attacking the guards and taking their weapons. The ship's mate was knocked down with a musket butt and beaten with an iron bar and a handspike. He later died and about 40 of the men escaped to Liverpool. On the following Wednesday one of the captured men was being taken to a boat but was freed by a mob. The mob went drinking and returned in the evening then broke open the watch-house and freed another impressed man after breaking the watch-master's ribs.

In 1779, the privateers *Ranger* of Bristol and the *Amazon* of Liverpool took the Spanish man-of-war, the *St.Inez* after an engagement of two hours. The *Amazon* was armed with 14 nine-pounders, and had a crew of 95 captained by Charles Whyttel. The *St. Inez* was laden with gold, silver, coffee, china, cochineal and indigo from Manilla for the King of Spain. The Spanish ship was taken into Cork badly damaged and the *Amazon* sailed to Hoyle Lake. A zebra shipped aboard the *St. Inez* in South Africa for the King of Spain was exhibited in Liverpool arousing great interest, as probably only the odd seafarer would have seen one before.

When ships accidentally ran aground or were wrecked in storms, local people stole the cargoes. As far as they were concerned it was 'finders keepers'. Accusations were made that Wirral people, particularly those living near the coast between Little Meols and Leasowe during the 1700s and early 1800s, were wreckers, deliberately luring ships onto the rocks and sandbanks, so to plunder the wrecks. There is no proof of this practice, which is correctly called wrecking, although often the word is used loosely, when the writer means wreck-looting.

Stonehouse wrote:
"Wirral up to the middle of the 18th century was a desperate region. The inhabitants were nearly all wreckers or smugglers. They ostensibly carried on the trade or calling of fishermen, farm labourers and small farmers. Many a fierce fire has been lighted on the Wirral shore on stormy nights to lure the good ship on the Burbo or Hoyle banks, there to beat and strain and throb, until her timbers parted, and her planks were floating in confusion on the stormy waves. On stormy days and nights, crowds might have been seen with carts, barrows, horses, asses and oxen even, which were made to draw timber, bales, boxes or anything that the raging waters might have cast up. Many a half-drowned sailor has had a knock on the sconce, whilst trying to obtain a footing, that has sent him reeling back into the seething water; and many a house has suddenly been replenished with eatables, drinkables and furniture - where previously bare walls and wretched accommodation were visible.
Then for smuggling: *fine times the runners used to have in my young days. Scarcely a house in North Wirral that could not provide a guest with a good stiff glass of brandy or Hollands.- Formby was a great place for smugglers. I don't think they wrecked as the Cheshire people did, these latter were perfect fiends".*

Certainly many a poor Wirral family must have become fairly rich and bought property and land with profits made from smuggling and wreck-looting. There are no eye-witness accounts of people lighting false signal fires or murdering shipwrecked sailors or passengers, but no doubt some bodies washed ashore were robbed.

A laden ship from St. Domingo called the *L' Equite* was being brought in when she ran aground off Dove Point and eventually lost her rudder. She was run ashore near New Ferry with her rich cargo intact. Hundreds of people from Wirral swooped down and forcibly seized and made off with large quantities of cargo. An armed guard was stationed on the ship which fired on the looters when they returned to plunder the ship again. The guard fired warning shots, then killed one of the crowd. The mob became so violent that the guard made off in a boat and left the ship's cargo to the looters. This account indicates that in this period a great many Wirral people were, in general, robbers.

A report written on the need for a Police Force in 1837, which includes a passage on wreckers, states that:- *"Chester and Cornwall are the worst. On the Cheshire coast not far from Liverpool, they will rob those who have escaped the perils of the sea and come safe on shore, and mutilate dead bodies for the sake of rings and personal ornaments"*.

The Commisioner of the Liverpool Police stated that; *"In Cheshire, parish constables never interfered with wreckers. The Borough police on salvage duty had to go armed against the hostility of neighbouring villagers"*.

One of my ancestors, farmer's son and cotton broker Charles Dawson Brown of Grange, was a well-known local historian, founder of Wirral's first museum and a founder member of the Royal Liverpool Golf Club. He recorded local information from many sources, much of it handed down through the family. His maternal grandfather and great grandfather had farmed in Moreton from the 1740s to the early 1800s. Also his mother's sister Mary Dawson was the wife of Bernard Sherwood, the Hoylake tide surveyor who, during the 1840s, lived at 5 Sea View, so that much authentic information was passed to Brown.

Looking from Red Rocks along the Dee coast to West Kirby and Caldy Hill.

The way Charles Dawson Brown wrote the following of wrecking in Wirral, he appears to mean wreck-looting of ships breaking up due to natural disasters, rather than people causing them to run aground:

There was a good deal of wrecking going on at one time, and when inward-bound West India ships met with disasters and broke up, a great gathering of men from the surrounding villages took place in order to secure casks of rum which came ashore, and which sometimes were buried in the sandhills, to be removed at a more convenient time. Deaths have frequently ensued from the heavy drinking of the strong new rum which took place at such times, and it has been frequently said that some of the casks which were buried have never been recovered. Happily, now, there are comparatively few wrecks, and wrecking is a thing of the past.

It is quite possible that some contraband hidden at night is still buried in the area. If, as Brown says, men 'sampled' some of the strong raw rum recovered from wrecks, then they probably staggered home their own separate ways like rubber giraffes. The next morning they would not know what day it was, let alone remember which sandhill or patch of scrub they had buried the loot in.

There was still no actual village of Hoylake but the name was becoming more popular and referred to the general area of Hoose and Little Meols.

The Tithe Apportionment of 1844 record John Stanley Lord of Alderley as the sole owner of the township of Little Meols, and his tennant farmers, fishermen and tradesmen were;

Armitage Joseph	Houghton James
Ball John	Little John
Ball Johnathan	Maddocks Joseph
Barlow Thomas	Overseers of the Township
Barton John	Parr Robert
Beck Robert	Powell Joseph
Buckley Philip	Pugh John
Croxton William	Rowland Thomas
Corporation of Liverpool	Silcox Thomas
Davies John	Thomas John
Hatton James	Welch Joseph
Hatton Sarah	Wharton Thomas
Hatton William	Williams Hugh
Holmes James	

In 1851 the townships of both Great and Little Meols were still small, each with a population of only 170, but the tiny township of Hoose sandwiched between the two Meols's had rocketed to 589. The reason for this was that at that time Lord Stanley would only *lease* land and property in Little Meols whereas in Hoose it was being *sold*. The old farming and fishing families were still the backbone of the communities.

Most of the fishermen (50) lived in Hoose, whilst only five lived in Little Meols. A good many of the fishermen lived in Lake Place which was partly in Hoose and partly in Little Meols, i.e. the boundary runs down the centre. The Hoose fishermen were born locally and christened in West Kirby parish except for Benjamin Evans and John Bythell of Neston, Thomas Steens of Heswall, John Eccles of Formby, John Fogg, and James Roberts of Liverpool, Peter Roberts of Bebington, George Smith of Bidston and Wilson Jones of Eastham. The Little Meols fishermen were all local except for Joseph Armitage who came from Bidston.

The Hoylake area has a great tradition of sea fishing. During the 1860s, '70s and '80s many of the men were employed on the deep-sea fishing boats, others fished inshore and gathered shellfish.

In 1885 Charles Dawson Brown wrote of Little Meols: *Little Meols separates the township of Hoose from that of West Kirby, and until 50 years ago could hardly be said to be a village, as with the exception of two hotels and two lighthouses, there were only a few thatched houses and cottages scattered over the township.*

There was fishing, shooting, boating and racing to be enjoyed. Horse racing on Little Meols common over a course of three miles was quite a popular event and gentlemen coming to watch stayed in the *Green Lodge* hotel.

Both Great and Little Meols were still mainly agricultural villages. During the 1870s, '80s and '90s, following the arrival of the railway in 1866, the already expanding population of Little Meols more than doubled in 10 years, from 926 in 1881 to 1,962 in 1891. Hoose and Great Meols had also greatly expanded, but Little Meols now had the biggest population of the three villages.

The newcomers called the area Hoylake as did the fishermen and the names of Little Meols and Hoose were used by very few people, mainly solicitors or local farmers.

People working in Liverpool, Birkenhead and Wallasey, who wanted to live in a rural seaside area, flocked to Hoylake and Meols when the new railway line made travel convenient and fast. Shops and trading premises sprang up to service these newcomers. Most people who settled in Little Meols during the 1880s and 1890s were not from Wirral, in fact they were from all over the world. There were only four public houses serving this large number of people.; the *Green Lodge, Royal Hotel, Stanley Hotel* and *The Letters*.

Elias Wolfgang a Hungarian wine broker and his Liverpool born wife Amey were recorded as living in Little Meols in 1881. Another business man from abroad was Henry D. Brandreth, an American merchant from New York who lived at *Espianga*, Stanley Road with his wife Addie and family.

The 1891 census records 312 families living within the boundaries of Little Meols, many with several servants. Few families were local. Of all these families, only one, the Ball's of Little Meols Road (now called Meols Drive) were recorded as being born in Little Meols. Families in which the husband and wife came from the same place include 10 born in Hoylake, which meant Little Meols or Hoose, one set of parents was from Great Meols, three from West Kirby, six from Birkenhead and 23 from Liverpool. Families with just the husband or wife born locally include two from Little Meols, 20 from Hoylake, one from Great Meols and three from West Kirby.

Most of these locals were the fishing families Armitage, Bird, Cooper, Eccles and Evans, living in Lake Place and Evans Road. Some had sons as young as 12 helping them work their boats. However it appears that Joseph Eccles was not impressed with the enthusiasm for fishing shown by his 12 year old son Joseph junior, whose occupation he registered as "an idler". Other locals working at various occupations were the old families of Ball, Cookson, Linekar, Little, Sherlock and Silcock.

The township of Little Meols was swamped with people from all over Britain and the world. To rich retired people, businessmen, shipowners and merchants, home life in a semi-rural area close to the sea with direct rail access to the city was very attractive. Some had quite a number of live-in servants, many of whom also came from far afield. Bakers, grocers, chemists, butchers, fishermen, chimney sweeps, painters and decorators etc., also made good livings in the Hoylake area.

The fact that people from far-flung unusual places chose to live in this small corner of Wirral speaks volumes for how popular and attractive the area was at the time. People came from Syria, Egypt, East India, Canada, U.S.A., Jamaica, British Guiana, Van Diemans Land,

Zanzibar, Brazil, Singapore, Switzerland, Peru and many other countries. Many people also came from Wales, Scotland and Ireland with 11 families coming from the Isle of Man.

This list is taken from the 1891 census and records some heads of families who came to live in the Little Meols area:

NAME	AGE	OCCUPATION	BORN
MARKET STREET.			
Jones William	69	Draper	Caerleon.
Iles Joseph	53	Baker & Confectioner	Liverpool.
Barnard Mary	46	Fancy Goods Dealer	London.
Ingham William	36	Ironmonger	Blackburn.
Singer John	48	Wine Merchants Manager	Warminster.
Peirce Francis	43	Medical Practitioner	Co. Limerick.
Bland William	37	Painter & Paperhanger	Liverpool.
ALDERLEY ROAD.			
Thexton Thos.	52	Photograper & Church Sexton	Westmorland.
Naiouy Gabriel	44	Publican	Aleppo, Syria.
Hoggarth Fred.	31	House Joiner	Clitheroe.
LAKE PLACE.			
Stanley Jas.	60	Plate Layer	Moreton.
CABLE ROAD.			
Soper Richard	62	Congrigational Minister	Grantham.
Ryder Thomas	69	Sailmaker	Liverpool.
PRUSSIA ROAD.			
Sprout James	57	Ship Owner	Scotland.
GROSVENOR ROAD.			
Harvey John	47	South American Merchant	Ireland.
Brewer Arthur	32	Watchmaker & Jeweller	Horncastle.
THOMAS ROAD.			
Butler William	24	Golf Club Maker	Ireland.
ALBERT ROAD.			
Haskins Arther	38	Hairdresser	Fenstanton.
AIRLIE ROAD.			
Blisset James	41	Gunmaker	Oxton.
DRUMMOND ROAD.			
Garside Thomas	58	Retired Police Officer	Lancashire.
KINGS GAP.			
Broomhall Geo.	34	Editor, Trade Newspaper	Madras India.
Brandreth Ad.	44		New York State
Pocock Julia	60	Living On Own Means (widow)	Lisbon, Portu.
WARREN ROAD.			
Kaye Arthur	36	Wine Merchant	Huddersfield
MARINE PARADE.			
Layborn Henry	37	Shipowner & Gen. Merchant	Eshe, Yorks.
Buggden Jane	68	Lets Apartments (widow)	Warrington.
LOWER LIGHTHOUSE.			
Codd James	42	Assistant Lighthouse Keeper	Pembrokeshire.
Askew James	40	Lighthouse & Telegr. Keeper	Liverpool.
STANLEY ROAD.			
Perrin Eugene	60	General Broker	Ireland.
Langlands Mat.	52	Steamship Owner	Ireland.
Travis Arthur	37	General Produce Broker	Liverpool.
Holford Edwin	38	Cotton Salesman	Liverpool.
Crowther Fred.	46	Chemical Merchant Director	Leeds.
LITTLE MEOLS ROAD.			
Blake Henry	36	Wholesale Stationer	Scotland.
Woodcock James	46	Chemist	Leicestershire

Johnston Carr.	66	Brazil Merchant	Bahia, Brazil.

LINGDALE ROAD.

Shone Robert	56	Iron Merchant	Harwarden.

RIVERSDALE ROAD.

Ackerley Eliza	62	(widow)	Ireland.
Baddeley Frank	52	Grocer	Salford.

BARTON ROAD.

Cowin William	47	Chimney Sweep	Laxey, I.O.M.

A typical prosperous Little Meols family of the 1890s, living in Riversdale Road is listed below in full:

McAfee William	35	General Practitioner	Ireland.
Elizab.	36		Scotland.
William	6		West Kirby.
Damean	4		West Kirby.
Lewis	2		West Kirby.
Nora	6 m.		West Kirby.
Grant Walter	10	(nephew)	Scotland.
McKeague John	27	Living on own Means (vis.)	Ireland.
Chapman Mary	36	Nurse & Domestic Servant	Luton.
Shett Sarah	23	Housemaid	Shropshire.
Lloyd Ada	20	Cook	Bootle.
Williams Frank	19	Page	Kirkdale.

(Vis. means visitor).

Chimney sweep William Cowin and his wife Isabella of Barton Road moved from the Isle of Man to Birkenhead in the 1870s. During the 1880s William and his family moved to Little Meols where there was great demand for men of his trade, owing to the large number of houses being built. Their son John James Cowin also became a chimney sweep and set up business at number 2 May Road, Heswall. To this day his descendants live in the Heswall area and I know the family well. The last Cowin to work as a chimney sweep was William's grandson the late Johnny Cowin, my dad's old mate. Johnny was a well liked Heswall character and a nice bloke to have a pint with. Johnny lived at 99 Pensby Road and still did a bit of sweeping during the 1970s.

Many families were large with several children and had other relations, visitors and servants living with them as can be seen by the McAfee household. One particularly large family was that of Americans Henry and Addie Brandreth, who had previously lived in other local areas including Liverpool, Bromborough and Oxton before settling in Little Meols. The 1891 census records 10 members of their family (including two American relations) and eight employees including servants, a governess and a nurse living in their house. On the day the census was recorded Mr. Henry Brandreth and two of his daughters, Eugenie and Virginia were not at home and could have been staying with relatives.

The name Brandreth is not a common one and my sister Geraldine wondered if the family in Little Meols was related to Gyles Brandreth, the Conservative M.P. for Chester. I wrote to Mr. Brandreth and he replied in a very interesting letter that he was indeed a direct descendant of this prosperous American family. His mother Mrs. Alice Brandreth has also written to me with fascinating information about her late husband's family, which enabled me to write the brief history below.

Dr. Brandreth of Liverpool used a vegetable concoction with great success among his poor patients in Liverpool during the early decades of the 1800s. From the the age of nine his grandson Benjamin Daubeney began helping him make the concoction. When he grew up Benjamin advertised in American papers and built up quite an export trade in Brandreth's Pills made from his grandfathers recipe. So, in 1835, aged 24, Benjamin emigrated to New York with his wife and three children to make their fortunes in the New World. He also took with him a plentiful supply of the family's well-established patent medicine, Brandreth's Pills, a simple laxative to you and me, but a powerful cure-all when marketed by Doctor Brandreth.

Benjamin Daubeney took his grandfather's name out of gratitude and was known in America as Benjamin Daubeney Brandreth of Ossining, New York, from Liverpool, England. He made a huge fortune from his pills and became a New York Senator with a splendid mansion on Fifth Avenue. Because of regular newspaper advertising the fame of his pills spread far and wide and by the time he died in 1880 the *New York Times* credited him with a personal fortune of a million dollars.

Benjamin's American born seventh son, Henry, had been sent over to Wirral in about 1870 to run the English end of the family business. Brandreth's Birkenhead factory was making money and exporting pills all over the world. After he had been in England a while Henry Daubeney Brandreth looked for a pleasant place to settle his family and eventually moved to the Little Meols area in the late 1870s, when he was in his early 30s. Unhappily, Henry appears to have eventually run the business into the ground and to have run through his own share of the family fortune too, by his extravagant life style.

Polly Brandreth, who works as a missionary in Africa, standing between two Californian Redwood trees at Pont-y-Pant. Henry Brandreth built the chapel behind and planted the two trees in 1900 as a memoriam to his two daughters who drowned there.

Henry and his wife Adeline Augusta (who was a born and bred American) had other houses in Wallasey, West Kirby and on Hilbre Island where they flew the American flag when staying there. They also leased *Lledr House*, Pont-y-Pant near Betws-y-Coed in Wales, which was used as a hunting lodge and was later to become a Youth Hostel.

On the morning of 10 August 1900, the Brandreth family were breakfasting on the lawn just above the River Lledr, across the road from *Lledr House*. Meanwhile Henry Brandreth accompanied by his gillie Mr. Roberts, was out shooting with some house guests up in the woods nearby when they heard screams below. They rushed down to find a scene of tragedy.

Somehow, 21 year old Virginia, and Eugenie, aged 23 had fallen into the River Lledr, possibly whilst having a bit of fun jumping from rock to rock. Their 17 year old brother Harry managed to pull one sister onto a rock while he went to rescue the other, but as he was doing so she slid off the rock and back into the river. Unfortunately, despite young Harry's desperate efforts, neither girl could be revived. Mr. Brandreth was heart broken and blamed himself for not being there. Virginia and Eugenie are buried at Pont-y-Pant.

Some years later Mr. Brandreth's eldest son Benjamin married and lived in Hoylake where his son Charles Daubeney was born in 1910. Benjamin also lived in Wales during the Great War where he served in the Home Guard and was put to guard the Menai Bridge. There was a shortage of rifles and he often recalled going on patrol armed with a hefty club.

Charles Daubeney Brandreth grew up to become a lawyer. He married Alice Addison, an extremely well educated young lady who was born in India and came to England to complete her law studies after taking two years of her Honours Course at the University of Toronto (Victoria College). In 1948 Alice and Charles had a son, Gyles. Today, Gyles Daubeney Brandreth, a former freelance journalist, theatrical producer, director and author of over 120 books, is the Conservative M.P. for Chester. The pill business in America still exists, in a very different guise, and is now run by one of Gyles' cousins.

Kelly's Directory of 1906 states the following of the area;
HOYLAKE is a watering place on the shore of the Irish Sea and near the estuary of the Dee, with a station on the Wirral Railway, 8 miles north west from Birkenhead. Hoylake-cum-West Kirby was formed into a civil parish in 1894 by Local Government Board Order No. 31,615 comprising within its area the former townships of Little Meols, Great Meols, Hoose and West Kirby, in the Wirral division of the county.

LITTLE MEOLS is a village, half a mile south from Hoylake station on the Wirral railway, and nine miles north west from Birkenhead, adjoining Hoose. Little Meols lighthouse, which stands on the shore, was built in 1865 by Mersey Docks and Harbour Board, it is 40 feet in height but is not illuminated. Lord Stanley of Alderley is lord of the manor and sole landowner. Soil, sandy; subsoil rocky.

HOOSE, an ancient township on the Irish Sea, which forms the central part of modern Hoylake, was formerly a small fishing village, the site of which, together with that of the township of Little Meols, is now covered with private residences; it is about half a mile north from Hoylake station on the Wirral railway and eight north west from Birkenhead, between Great Meols and Little Meols. The Wesleyan chapel here, built in 1886, is now used as a mission hall. The soil is sandy; subsoil, rocky.

GREAT MEOLS is a village on the Irish Sea, with a station on the Wirral railway, seven miles north west from Birkenhead. St. John the Baptist's church is a chapel of ease to Holy Trinity, Hoylake; it will seat 250 persons. The Presbyterian Church of England, erected in 1905, and seating 300 persons, is a branch of the one in West Kirby. Bertram Keightley esq. of Linden Gardens, London, is the principal landowner. Soil, sandy; subsoil, rocky. Chief crops are grass, wheat and potatoes.

Today Hoylake is a dormitory town and completely built up. In the area which was once Little Meols there are still a great many big houses which were the homes of Victorian shipowners and merchants. The area is very pleasant with the large open spaces of Hoylake Golf Course, the Royal Liverpool Golf Course and Carr Lane Fields on one side and the sea on the other. Pleasant walks can be had along the shore to Red Rocks or along Carr Lane past the sports grounds and across the fields to Newton.

"Over the line" is the local description for those roads on the other side of the railway lines, such as Harrington Avenue, strictly part of Hoose, and more particularly the Carr Lane estate in Little Meols, which is a mixture of private housing, sports grounds and small industrial units.

The word *carr* was originally an old Icelandic Viking word meaning fen, or boggy, or marshy land. The north end of Wirral is very low-lying, and prone to flooding, hence the constant efforts on sea defences.

The (technically mis-spelt) word *carrs*, (the correct plural of which is 'carse') appears regularly on older maps, virtually from Leasowe to Red Rocks. The lanes in these areas would have been difficult to traverse, a fact which is reputed to have been made good use of by wreck-looters and others anxious to avoid the Customs & Excise men.

It appears that all the lanes have at least two right-angle bends, so that they eventually end up at or near the intended destination, but those "not in the know" could get well and truly bogged down, never to appear again, if they simply headed in a direct line.

On the Carr Lane estate in Little Meols there are three distinct groups of road-names. The two paths called Carr Lane and New Hall Lane both show the characteristic double bends, and are clearly original footpaths.

Between the wars were built the mainly semi-detached houses with the odd bungalow, in the residential roads - Proctor Road, Edward Road, George Road and Yeoman Cottages.

The final group of road names, which begin with the letters car-, namely Carham, Carsgoe, Carsthorne and Carterton are apparently of recent date, as these are the roads forming the industrial area.

There seems to be something in Hoylake's sea air that attracts M.Ps. Apart from Gyles Brandreth M.P.s roots, we must not forget Selwyn Lloyd M.P., Glenda Jackson M.P. and David Hunt M.P.

INFORMATION

Local people. (Their memories, documents and letters etc.).
Census Returns.
Land Tax Documents.
Church Records.
Tithe Apportionments and Maps.
Directories.
Domesday Book, 1086.
Methodist Church Records, C.R.O. ref. EMS 134.
Brownbill, J., "West Kirby & Hilbre", Henry Young, 1928.
Cheshire Sheaf.
Sulley, P., "The Hundred of Wirral", B. Haram, 1889.
Hume, A., "Ancient Meols", John Russell Smith, 1863.
Old Newspapers.
Wirral Notes and Queries.
Transactions of Historic Society of Lancashire and Cheshire.
"The River Dee" [A guide to sources], Clwyd Record Office, 1987.
Howson, J.H., "River Dee", T.H.S.L.C., 1892.
Chester Archaelogical History Society., Parkgate, An Old Cheshire Port, 1911.
Williams G., "History of the Liverpool Privateers and Letters of Marque with an Account of the Liverpool Slave Trade", Heinmann, 1897.
Wedd, C.B., [et al] "Geology of Liverpool", Memoir of the Geological Survey, 1923.
O.S. and other plans.
(Including Bryants map of Wirral 1831, deposited in Cheshire Record Office and reproduced with permission of Cheshire County Council, to whom copyright is reserved).

REFERENCES

1. Cheshire County Council Archives and Local Studies, ref. DFI 176 page 124.

2. The original records and letters are stored in Northumberland Record Office, but copies are on microfiche in Cheshire Record Office, under "correspondence of John Watson re - Ness Colliery".

3. As 1, page 125. (From the Bishops Visitations and Transcripts recorded by W.F. Irvine between 1890 and 1900).

4. "Wirral Notes & Queries", 1892.

5. Ordnance Survey for County of Londonderry, page 36, as quoted by Hume.

GLOSSARY

Currency.
Until 15 February 1971 the English pound (L or £) was subdivided into shillings (s) and pence (d); £1 = 20s., 1s = 12d.

Land Measurement.
Since early times land has been measured in empirical terms: the amount of land which would support a family, the amount of land which could be ploughed in a given time, and so on. The Statute Acre of 4,840 square yards was defined by Edward I, although local measures persisted for centuries. The "large" or "Cheshire" acre was equal to two and one ninth statute acres. Both were subdivided into roods and perches; 1 acre = 4 roods, 1 rood = 40 perches.

Land Tax.
This was collected from 1692 to 1831, the usual rate being 4s. (20p) in the pound. The early lists of taxes collected usually only give names; later lists give more details such as a general description of the property.

Tithes.
In 1836 the tithes of farm produce and crops which the villagers paid to the Church were commuted into a monetary payment, and during the following decade a map and opportionment of all the fields and properties were drawn up for each village.

The importance of these records can be judged from the fact that they usually formed the earliest complete large-scale plan for a village, with the apportionments giving details of owners, occupiers, buildings, payments and sometimes crops in the field.

Place Names.
For convenience, the modern spelling of Meols has been used throughout; older sources sometimes use MEOLES. The north-east tip of Wales is called the Point Of Ayr, or Air, depending on which map you look at! For convenience, we have used Air.

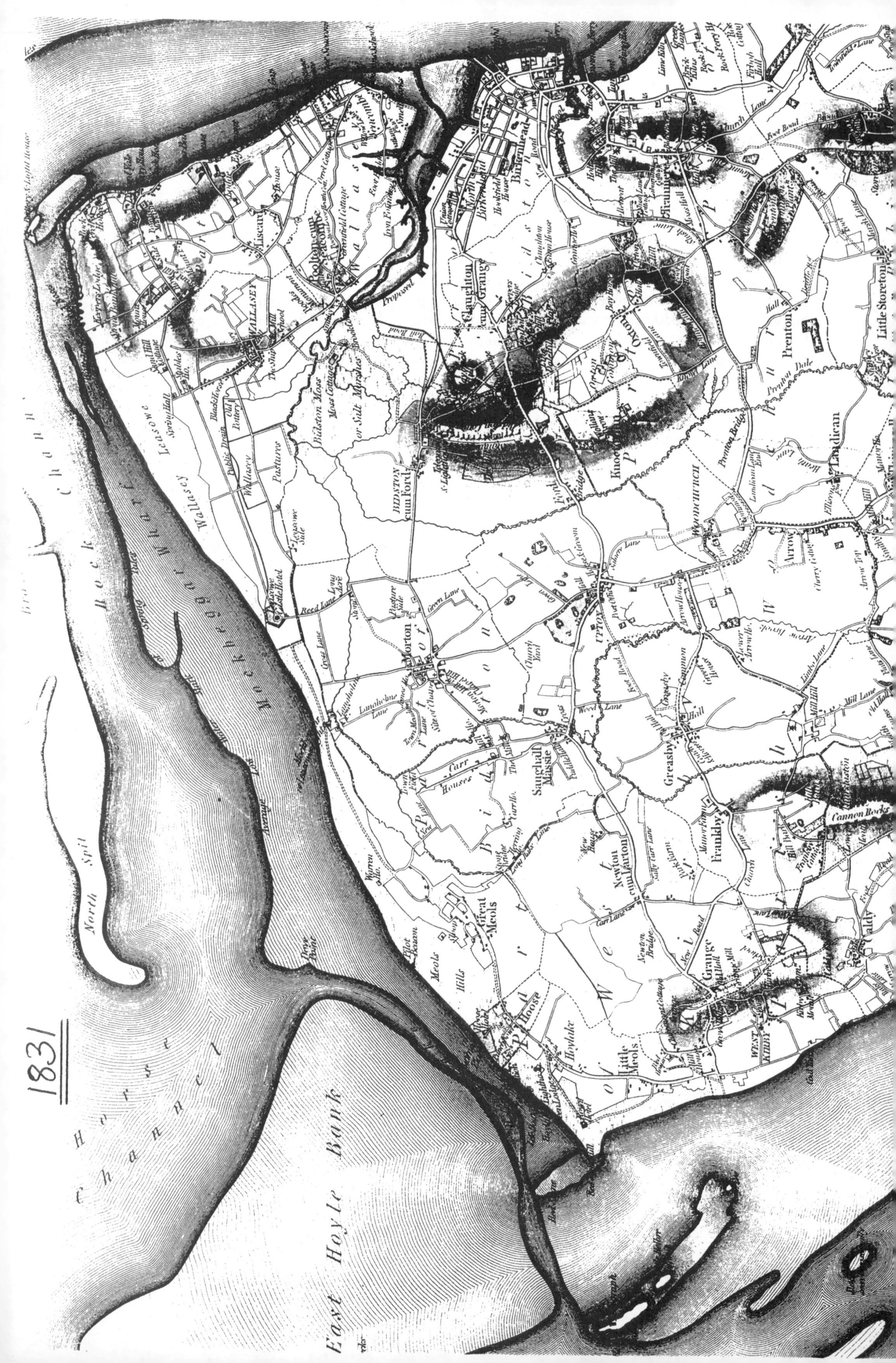

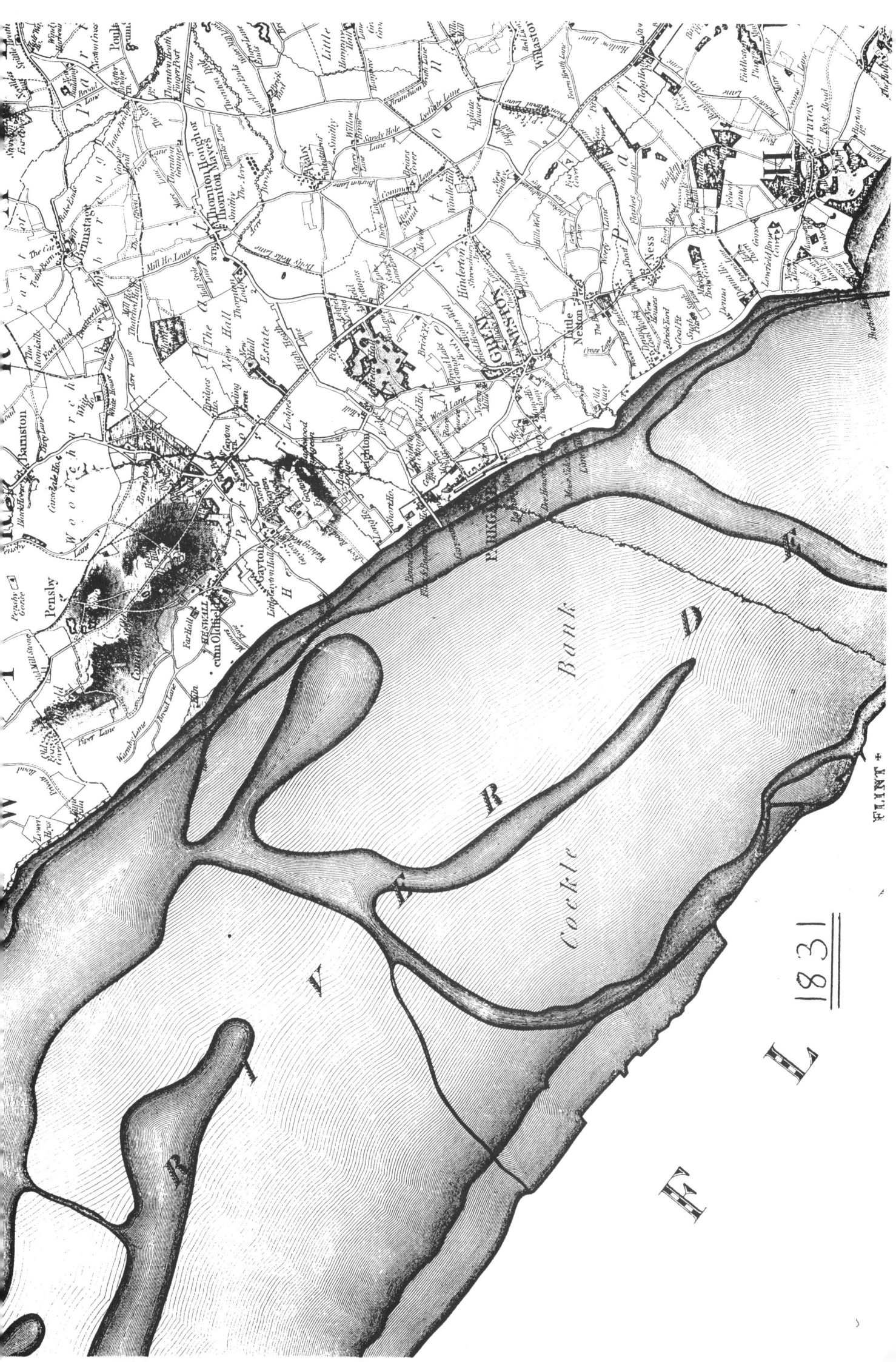

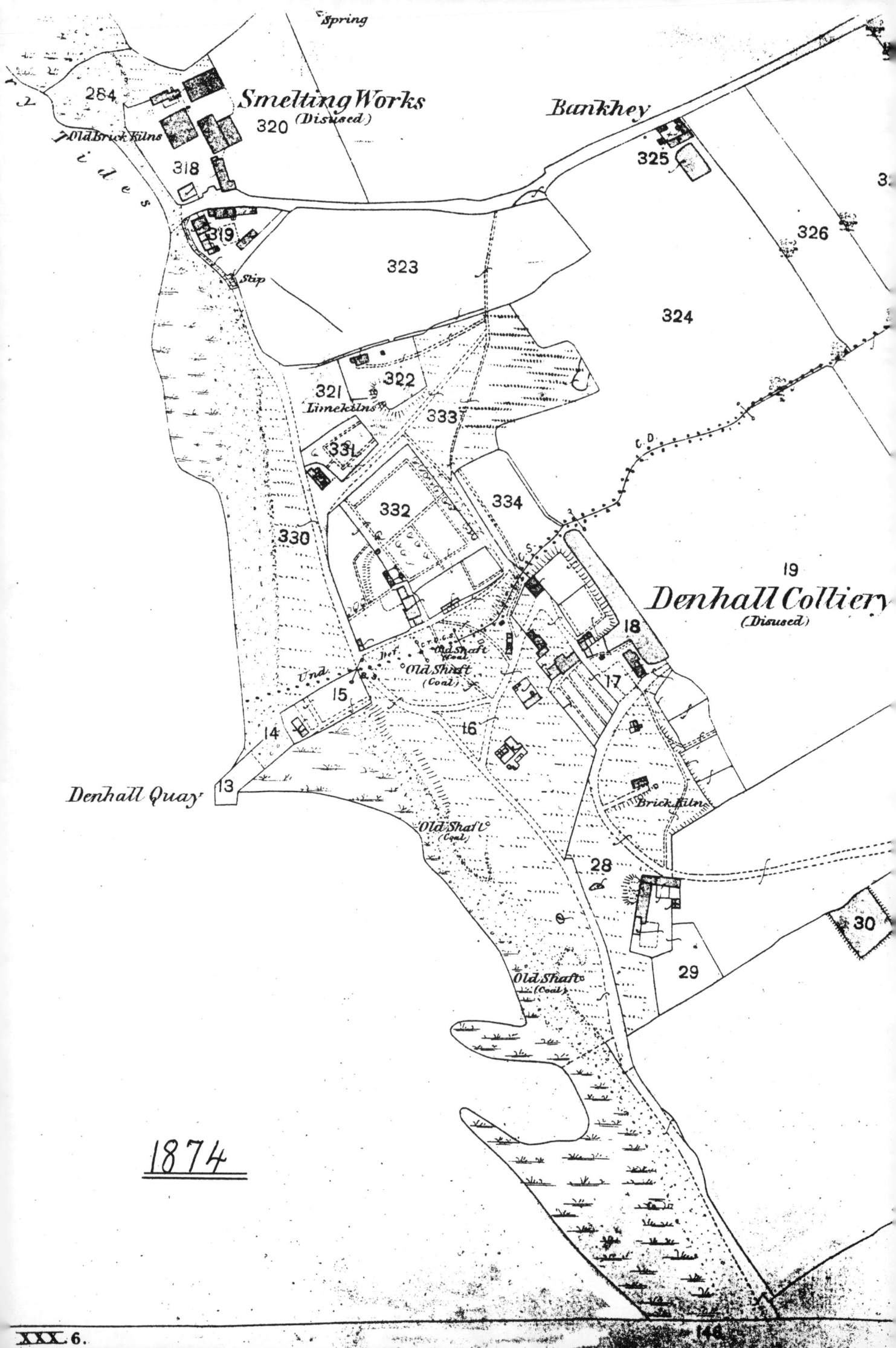

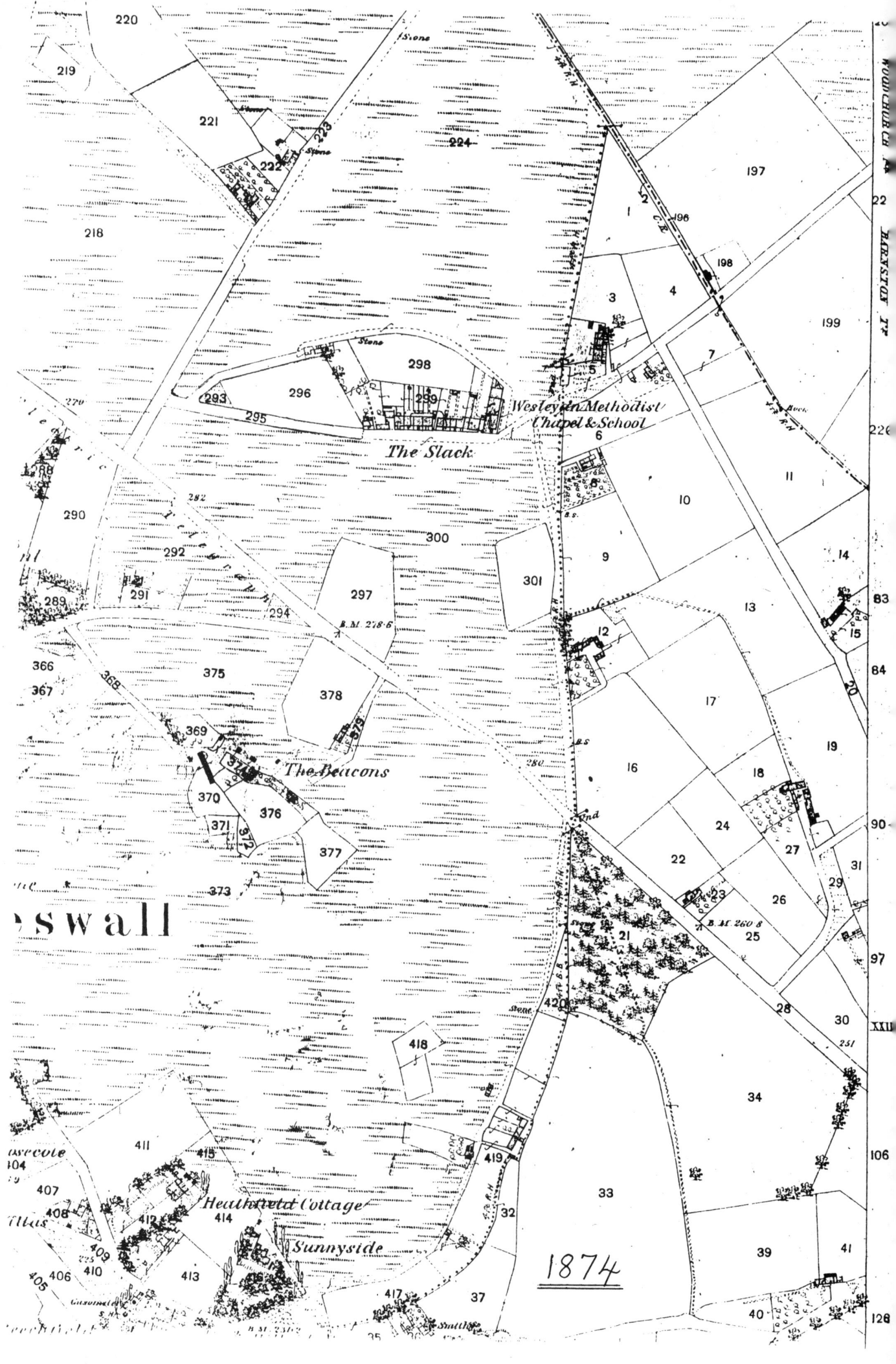